D1250001

Other books by Stephen Wilson

POETRY

Fluttering Hands

CRITICISM & PSYCHOLOGY

Poetics of the Diaspora

The Cradle of Violence:
Essays on Psychiatry, Psychoanalysis and Literature

The Bloomsbury Book of the Mind

Introducing the Freud Wars

BIOGRAPHY

Sigmund Freud: A Pocket Biography

STUDENT GUIDES

A Student Guide to Sigmund Freud

Isaac Rosenberg

Stephen Wilson

GREENWICH EXCHANGE
LONDON

Greenwich Exchange, London

Isaac Rosenberg

First published in Great Britain in 2010

Printed and bound by **imprint**digital.net
Typesetting and layout by Jude Keen, London
Tel: 020 8355 4541
Cover design by December Publications, Belfast
Tel: 028 90286559
Cover image: Self-Portrait Sketch in Steel Helmet
by Isaac Rosenberg reproduced with the kind permission
of Bernard Wynick and the Imperial War Museum.

Greenwich Exchange Website: www.greenex.co.uk

Cataloguing in Publication Data is available from the British Library.

ISBN: 978-1-906075-42-2

for my grandson, Jonah, with love

Contents

Acknowledgements

I owe many thanks to Bernard Wynick, Isaac Rosenberg's nephew, who generously gave permission to quote from work that remains in copyright. This includes material in both *Isaac Rosenberg: The Collected Works* published by Chatto & Windus, reprinted by permission of The Random House Group Ltd., and *Isaac Rosenberg: Poetry Out of My Head and Heart* published by Enitharmon and reprinted with its permission. He also kindly helped with other queries. Similarly Joan Rodker, Sonia Cohen's daughter, gave permission to quote from her mother's unpublished memoirs, written under her married name of Sonia Joslen. I am grateful to the Ben Uri Gallery for facilitating communication with Ms Rodker. For information on Rosenberg's life I have drawn principally on the biographies of Joseph Cohen and Jean Moorcroft Wilson. She and Cecil Woolf also took the trouble to answer questions. Shirley Zangwill graciously allowed me to quote from her father-in-law's letters. Siegfried Sassoon's comments are quoted copyright Siegfried Sassoon by kind permission of the Estate of George Sassoon. Joseph Leftwich's diary (1917) is held by the Imperial War Museum. His memoir on Rosenberg (1939) is held in the Central Zionist Archives (CZA A 330/595 p.13), to whom I am grateful for permission to quote. Laurence Binyon is quoted by permission of the Society of Authors, Literary Representatives of the Estate of Laurence Binyon. The correspondence between Ezra Pound and Harriet Monroe is quoted with permission of the University of Chicago Library. Every effort has been made to trace copyright holders. Any whom I have failed to find will be happily acknowledged in future editions. As always I owe an immeasurable debt to my wife, Kate Wilson.

Chronology

1887 Dovber Rosenberg, Isaac's father, arrives in England from Russia.

1888 Hacha Rosenberg and Minnie, Isaac's mother and sister, arrive in England.

1890 November 25th, Isaac is born in Bristol.

1897 Family (with five children, soon to be six) moves to Cable Street, East End, London.

1899 Isaac sent to Baker Street School, Stepney, where headmaster Usherwood takes a special interest in him.

1900 Family makes first of several moves in Jubilee Street, Stepney. Isaac introduced to artist John Amshewitz and Miss Winifreda Seaton.

1902 Begins classes at Arts and Crafts School, Stepney Green.

1905 Apprenticed to Carl Hentschel, a Fleet Street engraver.

1907 Commences evening classes at Birkbeck College. Tutored by Miss Alice Wright. Wins prizes.

1908 Meets Mark Gertler, David Bomberg, Mark Weiner and Sonia Cohen in Whitechapel Library.

1911 Meets Joseph Leftwich, Samuel Winsten and John Rodker. Joins 'Whitechapel Group'. Leaves Hentchel's. Meets Lily Delissa Joseph and is taken on as tutor to her son. Introduced to patrons, Mrs Henrietta Löwy and Mrs Herbert Cohen. Registers at Slade School.

1912 Writes to and meets Laurence Binyon. Prints *Night and Day*. Falls out with Mrs Cohen.

1913 Meets Annetta Raphael. Holidays with Bomberg on Isle of Wight. Sister Minnie marries and emigrates to South Africa. Meets Edward Marsh and T.E. Hulme at Café Royal.

1914 Leaves Slade. Sails for South Africa. Meets Margueretha Van Hulsteyn, Ruth Alexander, Madge and Agnes Cook, Betty Molteno. Gives lectures on art. Publishes 'Beauty' and 'Our Dead Heroes' in *South African Women in Council.* WAR DECLARED. Spends fortnight at Molteno's home in Rondebosch.

1915 Returns to live with family at Dempsey Street, Stepney, their permanent home after numerous moves. Prints *Youth.* Fails to obtain work at Henschel's. Meets Sydney Schiff. Ezra Pound sends Rosenberg's poems to Harriet Monroe. Enlists in army.

1916 Reuben (Crazy) Cohen prints *Moses.* Rosenberg Embarks for France. Arrives at front. Receives encouraging letters from Georgian poets, Lascelles Abercrombie, Gordon Bottomley and R.C. Trevelyan. Sends 'Break of Day in the Trenches' to Harriet Monroe, editor *Poetry.* She prints it together with 'Marching' previously sent by Rodker.

1917 Re-assigned 40th Division Works Battalion, behind lines. Re-assigned 229 Field Co., Royal Engineers, attached to 11th Batallion, King's Own Royal Lancasters. 10 days home leave. Marsh publishes 'Ah Kolue' in *Georgian Poetry.* Sick with influenza, hospitalised 51st General Hospital. Returns to trenches mid December.

1918 April 1st, killed in action.

Posthumous publications

1922 *Selected Poems* edited by Gordon Bottomley, published by William Heinemann.

1937 *Collected Works* edited by Gordon Bottomley and Denys Harding, published by Chatto & Windus.

1979 *Collected Works* including poetry, prose, letters, paintings and drawings edited by Ian Parsons published by Chatto & Windus.

2004 Poems, plays and comprehensive bibliography edited by Vivien Noakes, published by Oxford University Press.

2007 Manuscripts and previously unpublished letters edited by Jean Liddiard, published by Enitharmon Press.

2008 *Complete Works* edited by Vivien Noakes, published by Oxford University Press.

Introduction

I go to meet Moses who assuredly was a suicide,
and the young Christ who invited death,
I who have striven to preach the gospel of beauty—

I.R

Born in 1890 to an impoverished family of Russian Jewish immigrants, son of a father who fled his homeland to escape conscription, brought up speaking Yiddish as his mother tongue, lacking in education, short in stature and social grace, inferior in social class and military rank, introverted to a fault, Isaac Rosenberg is perhaps the most unlikely of war poets. Yet his compelling imagery (one can never forget he was a painter-poet), his innovative language and emotional intensity, his unflinching eye, place him among the greatest English poets of the First World War. 'Break of Day in the Trenches', written in 1916, is a fine example of his rich and wry and overwhelmingly human work. The poem describes a rat with "cosmopolitan sympathies" that crosses between German and English lines. It is a beautifully crafted piece of subversion. Seen through the rat's eyes, the human combatants appear frail and foolish. Litotes (understatement) can scarcely have been employed to better poetic effect:

The darkness crumbles away.
It is the same old druid Time as ever,
Only a live thing leaps my hand,
A queer sardonic rat,
As I pull the parapet's poppy
To stick behind my ear.
Droll rat, they would shoot you if they knew

Your cosmopolitan sympathies.
Now you have touched this English hand
You will do the same to a German
Soon, no doubt, if it be your pleasure
To cross the sleeping green between.
It seems you inwardly grin as you pass
Strong eyes, fine limbs, haughty athletes,
Less chanced than you for life,
Bonds to the whims of murder,
Sprawled in the bowels of the earth,
The torn fields of France.
What do you see in our eyes
At the shrieking iron and flame
Hurled through still heavens?
What quaver—what heart aghast?
Poppies whose roots are in man's veins
Drop, and are ever dropping;
But mine in my ear is safe—
Just a little white with the dust.

Artillery shells raked the earth on the desolate battlefields of the Western Front providing ideal growing conditions for the corn poppy. Rosenberg's inspired use of the flower as a symbol of spilt blood antedated its adoption by the British Legion for Remembrance Day five years later. But it has taken nearly a century for Rosenberg himself to begin to achieve the sort of recognition accorded to Wilfred Owen, Edward Thomas, Rupert Brooke, Edmund Blunden, Siegfried Sassoon and other contemporaries. Sassoon, writing in 1937, acknowledges Rosenberg's genius – "Scriptural and sculptural are the epithets I would apply to him," he says, and "His experiments were a strenuous effort for impassioned expression; his imagination had a sinewy and muscular aliveness; often he saw things in terms of sculpture, but he did not carve or chisel; he *modelled* words". In fact Rosenberg's reputation has grown as that of the others in his generation faded. Sandwiched between the strict classicism of the Victorian era and the Modernist rejection of form, Georgian poets have little appeal to the twenty-first-century ear. But although Rosenberg's mentors were committed 'Georgians' – their influence can be seen in his treatment of grand Biblical themes, verse plays, and tendency toward the orotund in earlier work – the force driving his poetry was unimpeachably unique. It was, ultimately, immune to deformation by well-intentioned critics. Where poetry was concerned he was an autodidact, seeking recommendations from friends wherever he could and satisfying his need through long hours spent pouring over books in the

Whitechapel Library. It is as if inside a thin carapace of conventional prosody, a Modernist intent on syntactical innovation, precise diction and direct expression of 'the thing', could not be prevented from breaking out.

Rosenberg was nearly twenty-five years old when he unexpectedly volunteered for service at the end of October 1915, and twenty-seven and a half on April 1st 1918, when he voluntarily returned to the front line during a period of respite from fighting, and was killed in action. In the intervening period he somehow managed to write and send home more than thirty poems and three verse plays, and to keep up a regular correspondence with family and friends. Certainly he had a lust for life, writing from the trenches to his mentor, Laurence Binyon, in autumn 1916:

> I am determined that this war, with all its powers for devastation, shall not master my poeting; that is, if I am lucky enough to come through all right.

But against this, one cannot help thinking there was a death-wish at work that eventually overpowered him. An undated prose fragment redolent of Keats' 'Nightingale' demonstrates his identification with two Jews, Moses and Jesus, both of whom he sees as having embraced death; and there is an undoubted preoccupation with self-destruction:

> If I could die and leave no trace, ah, that thought of mine must live, incomplete and imperfect, maimed. Could I destroy all I have ever thought and done.

One can see the foreshadowing of Dylan Thomas' 'And Death Shall Have No Dominion', when Rosenberg writes, "Death does not conquer me, I conquer death, I am the master". These words take on a deeper meaning when we consider they come from a man whose elder twin died at birth. There is nothing glib in the idea that the emotional conflict such an experience engenders, a complex mix of triumph, loss, guilt, and compassion, fuels the creative urge. Thornton Wilder, just seven years younger than Rosenberg, another twin who survived his brother's death, ruminated obsessively on the theme and introduced it into nearly everything he wrote. The need to be reunited with a lost twin is, perhaps, a desire that can only be accomplished in death.

War did not make Rosenberg into a poet, rather Rosenberg made the war serve his poetic purposes – he had been writing poems since the age of ten or twelve. And though his juvenilia are in many ways derivative, they bear the unmistakeable stamp of the *word-modelling* to which Siegfried Sassoon refers

– "a hill-ensceptred Queen" – "that robe with woof of glory" – "Above the monstrous mass that seethed and flowed / Through one of London's nights" (which surely presages T.S. Eliot's "A crowd flowed over London Bridge") – "Lost in promiscuous bewilderment, / Which to my mazèd soul was wonder-food".[1] By the time he joined the army Rosenberg had already produced outstandingly innovative work, for example 'Midsummer Frost' probably written in early 1914 whose opening stanza reads:

> A July ghost, aghast at the strange winter,
> Wonders, at burning noon, (all summer seeming),
> How, like a sad thought buried in light words,
> Winter, an alien presence, is ambushed here.

Rosenberg is, above all, a poet of the Anglo-Jewish Diaspora. If his material circumstances were impoverished, his Hebrew cultural heritage was rich, and formed a productive growth medium into which English language and literature were injected. This is not to say the fusion was without conflict. Given the history of the Jewish people that would be impossible. On the contrary, experience of the early twentieth-century English Diaspora is better regarded as grit in the matrix of Rosenberg's Jewishness. As he recoiled from the constraints of traditional Judaism, and the slights of traditional English anti-Semitism, he found sympathetic gentiles to induct him into the world of art and literature – a world where ancient Hebrews were romanticised and living ones anathematised.

Jews had been institutionally demonised since the fourth century when Christianity became the official religion of the Roman Empire (and Jews, not Romans, the official killers of Christ). Driven out of their homeland of Israel in the second century, massacred in Germany and France during the Crusades, expelled from England in the thirteenth century, from Spain at the end of the fifteenth, slaughtered in Poland during the mid seventeenth, banished from France between the sixteenth and eighteenth centuries up until the Revolution, forcibly baptized in Portugal, fleeing from Czarist Russia in the nineteenth (and as we know subject to Nazi genocide in the twentieth); it made little difference whether the host country was Catholic, Orthodox or Protestant, Jews were restricted and reviled. The growth of modern liberal democracy meant that Rosenberg's generation faced few civil impediments in England, but 'social' anti-Semitism remained both acceptable and widespread. As a private soldier it is certain he experienced his fair share of it. "How odd of God / To choose the Jews," quipped the British journalist William Norman Ewer, and Rosenberg's poem, 'The Jew' could be taken as a wearisome rejoinder:

Moses, from whose loins I sprung,
Lit by a lamp in his blood
Ten immutable rules, a moon
For mutable lampless men.

The blonde, the bronze, the ruddy,
With the same heaving blood,
Keep tide to the moon of Moses,
Then why do they sneer at me?

Little wonder that early Zionism was widely embraced as a movement of national liberation that would transform Zion, the historical and spiritual home of the Jews, into a satisfactory temporal one. Israel Zangwill, an established writer to whom Rosenberg sent his earliest poems, expressed the existential conflict thus:

Risking our lives for our countries, loving our nation's flags,
Hounded therefrom in repayment, hugging our bloody rags

[...]

Hear, O Israel, Jehovah, the Lord our God is One,
But we, Jehovah His people, are dual and so undone.

And Rosenberg's first youthful poem (possibly written as early as 1900 or 1902), 'Ode to David's Harp', voices the traditional lament at exile evident from the Psalms, through the tenth century Hispano-Jewish poets up until modern times:

Awake! ye joyful strains, awake!
In silence sleep no more;
Disperse the gloom that ever lies
O'er Judah's barren shore.

His last one, written some fifteen years later, echoes the theme. In August, 1917, a unique unit in the British Army, a battalion of Jewish soldiers known as the *Judeans*, was raised by the Government in order to serve in Palestine and participate in what proved to be a successful campaign against the Turks. Rosenberg's friend, the sculptor Jacob Epstein, was in it. In a final letter from the trenches, written to his patron, Edward Marsh, and posted the day *after* he was killed, Rosenberg complains about the lack of news regarding his application for a transfer; and characteristically in the same breath, the damage done to his vocabulary by prolonged separation from poetry – small enough before, it has now become "impoverished and bare". He had wanted to write a battle song for the *Judeans* but can think of nothing strong and wonderful enough so encloses 'Through these pale cold days' which he describes as "a slight thing":

> Through these pale cold days
> What dark faces burn
> Out of three thousand years,
> And their wild eyes yearn,
>
> While underneath their brows
> Like waifs their spirits grope
> For the pools of Hebron again—
> For Lebanon's summer slope.
>
> They leave these blond still days
> In dust behind their tread
> They see with living eyes
> How long they have been dead.

NOTE:

1 'In Zion' (1906) and 'A Ballad of Whitechapel' (1910) in Selected Additional Poems at the end of this book.

1

Forebears

One-third of the Jews must die, one-third emigrate, and one third assimilate.

Pobedonostzev, Ober-Procurator of the Holy Synod
(1827-1907)

In 1881 Czar Alexander Nikolaevich II, Emperor and Autocrat of all the Russias, King of Poland and Grand Duke of Finland was assassinated. Among the group of six revolutionaries subsequently rounded up was Hessia Helfman, a Jewish woman who helped rent the headquarters for the conspiracy. One assassination doesn't make a revolution. It was to be a further thirty-six years before the Bolsheviks seized power in October 1917, but the event acted as a more immediate trigger for the scapegoating and persecution of millions of Helfman's co-religionists.

Russia had never been kind to its Jews who were perceived as Christ-killers and a threat to the fabric of Orthodox Christian society. But as Russian Czars pushed westward in the seventeenth and eighteenth centuries conquering territory in Poland, Estonia, and Lithuania, an increasing number came under their rule. By the end of the nineteenth century there were over five million Jews living in Imperial Russia representing approximately 5% of the general population. Most were confined by Catherine the Great to the Pale of Settlement, an area between the Baltic and Black Sea, where they were subject to discriminatory legislation and the fear of periodic pogroms. Until the mid-1850s Jewish boys from the age of twelve (in practice some as young as eight) were pressed into twenty-five years service in the Russian army, where they were supposed to be educated, assimilated and 'modernised'. Towards the end of the century the duration of military service had been reduced to five years. Nonetheless Jews were conscripted into the army in disproportionate numbers by comparison with their non-Jewish countrymen. It meant forcible separation from culture and tradition, inability to practice their religion, subjection to a prejudicial regime intent on conversion, and bullying and harassment from other soldiers. It remained a huge threat to Jewish identity.

Alexander's succession to the throne had marked the onset of a temporary period of liberalisation and opportunity. But following his demise Jews were to feel the full force of popular Russian anti-Semitism, manipulated as a diversionary political weapon by a crumbling despotism. Anti-Jewish riots broke out and continued sporadically over the years where looting, murder and rape occurred. In 1882 the infamous May Laws were enacted cancelling the freedoms that Alexander had introduced. Jews were prohibited from land ownership in rural areas, brutally expelled from towns and villages where they had been living, and their ability to participate in civil society was drastically curtailed. "To lock people like wild beasts in a cage, to surround them with disgraceful laws, as in an immense circus, for the sole revolting purpose to let loose the murderous mob upon them whenever practicable for St. Petersburg – terrible, terrible!", declared Leo Tolstoy in outrage.

Of the millions who fled the country in the closing decades of the nineteenth century, by far the greatest proportion ended up in America, widely known in the Yiddish-speaking world as 'Die Goldene Medina (The Golden Land)', but well over a hundred thousand found their way to Britain where they remained, either because they lacked funds for the onward passage or because their kinsfolk were already ensconced. Among them was Dovber Rosenberg (later known as Barnard or Barnett) who arrived in 1887, to be joined a year later by his wife, Hacha, and baby daughter, Minnie. Like many he came penniless, steeped in Hebrew culture, unable to speak English, and ill-equipped both by temperament and tradition to make his way in the British economy. Far from finding anything resembling a golden land, they arrived at a time when the British Chief Rabbi, Nathan Marcus Adler, was pleading with his East European colleagues to discourage emigration. In a circular letter issued in 1888, he appealed to:

> Every Rabbi of a community kindly to preach in the Synagogue and house of study, to publicise the evil which is befalling our brethren who have come here, and to warn them not to come to the land of Britain, for such ascent is a descent.

During the same year, mounting opposition to the influx of immigrant paupers saw the appointment by Parliament of a Select Committee of Enquiry into Alien Immigration. And the 'Jack the Ripper' murders in Whitechapel provided a focus for 'Judophobia'. After the third one on the 16th September, the Editor of the *East London Observer* under the heading: 'A Riot against the Jews' recorded:

> On Saturday in several quarters of East London the crowds who assembled in the streets began to assume a very threatening attitude towards the Hebrew population of the District. It was repeatedly asserted that no Englishman could have perpetrated such a horrible crime as that of Hanbury Street, and that it must have been done by a JEW – and forthwith the crowds began to threaten and abuse such of the unfortunate Hebrews as they found in the streets. Happily the presence of a large number of police prevented a riot actually taking place.

It was not simply a case of 'Out of the frying pan into the fire'. England was no automatic gateway to prosperity, but it was also not Russia. It remained a haven of freedom in the minds of most East European Jews. They knew it to be a place where (at that time) military conscription was frowned upon, popular anti-Semitism was not supported by the government, and civil rights were increasingly available to all citizens. And at the age of twenty-five, Dovber Rosenberg's ability to bribe his way out of the Russian army had run out. From his own account it would appear he had been trying to escape military service for at least ten years, since his father first unsuccessfully attempted to buy off local officials by causing "silver and gold to flow".

The third of four sons from his father Hezek's second marriage (there were two half-sisters from the first), Dovber was born in a country inn just outside the small village of Shtat in the province of Kovno, Lithuania. Raised in a Levite family of scholars and rabbis he was himself, like his older brother Peretz, destined for the rabbinate. Indeed his name, a tautological combination of the Hebrew and Yiddish words for bear, derived from one of the founding fathers of the Hasidic movement which had spread rapidly through the Jewish community in the eighteenth century. It was a reaction against empty ritualism and academic Talmud study that emphasised spiritual development and joyful attachment to religion.

Dovber's happy childhood, spent in the bucolic surroundings of Shtat, was etched into, and perhaps idealised, in his memory. Years later, in 1915, he composed a poem in Yiddish entitled, 'This Was My Youth', celebrating snow-capped mountain peaks, blue skies, green grass, stately firs and placid streams. And he remembered being carried on the shoulders of a family servant for a fishing expedition in early spring.

As is traditional in orthodox Jewish families he began his Hebrew studies at the age of five. They were congenial enough, but as he grew older a way of enabling him to continue his training for the rabbinate and avoid military service had to be found. When it became clear that local draft officials had pocketed his father's sweetener without keeping their side of the bargain, an alternative course of action was urgently required. To this end he was moved to Kreitzburg, a small town in the province of Vitebsk, later depicted in the paintings of Marc Chagall, where a relative arranged for him to live in the synagogue and continue his studies unbeknown to the authorities. However, he had no papers and as a hidden Jew remained vulnerable to discovery. Eventually, with the help of two hundred roubles sent by his father, he managed to purchase forged identity documents, but he was advised to move on.

Accordingly he relocated to Dünaburg (later Dvinsk), where he reluctantly took on the role of Hebrew teacher, the only job he considered himself fit to do, that carried with it the perk of living in the house of the chief community worthy. It was a truth universally acknowledged among his people that a single man *not* in possession of a good fortune must be in want of a wife. And it took little persuasion on the part of his host to arrange a marriage between young Dovber and Hacha (Hannah) Davidov, the daughter of a local innkeeper. It pushes the limits of belief to suggest, as Dovber later did in an autobiographical fragment, that her family were aristocrats who had fallen on hard times, but they did possess their own cow. Moreover she was not unattractive, interested in the arts, occasionally composed verse and was skilled in the preparation of herbal medicines. Unfortunately for her new husband, she was also headstrong and shrewish. She did not accept the customary marital compact for a 'Talmud hocham' (a man who devoted himself to religious study), whereby his wife forwent expectations of material support, and she came to perceive him as a feckless dreamer. She was also in love with another man, a cousin whom she had been forbidden to marry. When the promised dowry failed to materialise, the stage was set for a lifetime of rancorous cohabitation.

Still travelling on papers that had to be 're-forged' on an annual basis, Dovber and his wife now made for Moscow where he took a job in his brother-in-law's department store. When the first baby, Minnie, arrived in 1881, he decided to branch out on his own and, with no prior skill in meat-cleaving, opened a butcher's shop. Surprisingly the enterprise went well until one night he was raided by the police – someone must have informed them of his illegal status. Unable to produce his permit for living in Moscow he was arrested and summarily imprisoned. His shop was subsequently confiscated, and he was released on condition that he left the city. Hacha, however, because she was caring for an infant, was allowed (and opted) to stay with her brother. Since she was on the point of seeking divorce, the enforced separation may not have been entirely unwelcome.

Dovber's fugitive odyssey now took him eastward, where he hoped to live incognito and find work, eventually reaching the town of Azzia in Siberia. But by the end of 1885 when he failed to receive revalidated papers after sending off money, he knew the game was up. Rather than wait for the authorities in Shtat to find him, he made his way back to Lithuania and thence, having slipped quietly across the German border, to Hamburg. Freed from Russian persecution he intended to traverse the Atlantic and find the Goldene Medina. His point of disembarkation, however, could not have been further from his dreams, not New York but the north-eastern English fishing port of Hull!

A newly-landed immigrant, estranged from his wife and daughter, living on his own in a far off country, guided by Jewish charities, Dovber made his way to Leeds, where he drifted from job to job with little enthusiasm. He managed to get sacked from a tailor's shop by burning the clothes he was supposed to be pressing, tried peddling but was put off by the winter weather, worked temporarily as an overseer in a slaughter-house and when the season changed moved south-west. In the milder climate he once again took to the road selling shoes from door to door, travelling through Bristol, Cornwall, Devon and the Isle of Wight. Meanwhile, Hacha, having decided that she could not rely on her brother indefinitely and life as a single mother was unsustainable, decided to rejoin her husband. No longer a runaway from the Czar's army, Dovber was now being actively sought by his wife and child who had arrived in England determined to locate him.

If he had seemed destined to fulfil the role of 'Wandering Jew' allotted by Christian mythology, it was not to be. Reunited in 1888, the Rosenbergs made a home in the Temple district of Bristol, where they stayed for the next nine years. Hacha sold embroidery and took in sewing while Dovber (having adopted the name of Barnett) continued his seasonal work as a licensed hawker. They went on to produce a family of six children, two more girls and three boys, the eldest of whom, Isaac, was born on November 25, 1890, the only survivor of a twin pregnancy.

2

Boyhood

You mustn't forget the circumstances I have been brought up in, the little education I have had.

I.R.

Bristol in the 1890s was a vibrant city with a growing population that reached 330,000 by the end of the decade. Brunel's Great Western Railway linking it with London in a journey time of just four hours had opened in 1841. His revolutionary transatlantic liner, the SS *Great Britain*, was launched two years later providing luxury travel from Bristol to North America and the Clifton Suspension Bridge was completed in 1864. In 1879 the first telephone exchange was opened. Shipbuilding boomed as did the tobacco, chocolate and cotton industries based on local imports. In 1893 the city mounted an Industrial and Fine Arts Exhibition held in a specially built wooden hall that featured an electric clock. It lasted five months and drew in half a million people.

Men in bowler hats and boaters, women in long skirts, children in sailor suits, horse-drawn trams, hansom cabs and four-wheeled flys thronged the streets. Gas lamps lit them. The first electric tram was introduced in 1895. There was a Zoo Garden where flower shows were held, trapeze artists performed, bands played, and a famous elephant, Zebi, gave rides to children. Boat trips on the lake were provided as well as tennis, croquet and archery.

But it is doubtful Isaac Rosenberg, living in a poor overcrowded house, raised in the narrow streets and alleys of the dockside, ever enjoyed these amenities. His father was absent from home for long stretches and the profits from peddling were meagre. With a growing family to feed, the money his busy mother brought in from sewing only just made ends meet. And as the son of newly-arrived Jewish immigrants, his social life was circumscribed. Two of his uncles (Barnett's brothers) lived nearby but the Jewish community in Bristol was small. To be sure there had been a presence in the twelfth century that was re-established in the 1750s, a new synagogue was opened in 1880 and a Hebrew school founded in the year of Isaac's birth, but the Rosenbergs' name does not appear in local synagogue records. It is likely that the family was culturally isolated, separated from the established Anglo-Jewish community by a divide almost as large as that between themselves and their Gentile working-class neighbours.

The 1870 Education Act enabled local Boards to use rate-payers' money for the provision of elementary schools in their area. By 1880 there were enough to make attendance compulsory for all children between the ages of 5 and 10. Isaac would therefore have commenced his education in 1895. However his mother was becoming increasingly dissatisfied with life in Bristol. In February 1897 she gave birth to a son, David, to join Minnie, Isaac, Annie and Rachel. There were now seven mouths to feed (soon to be eight after Elkon was born in 1899) and many of her friends who might have given succour had left the area. When the Levine family who lived next door departed for London and sent back positive reports, she determined to join them in the large East End Jewish community. The move, it was thought, would also enable seven-year-old Isaac to join the Jews' Free School in Spitalfields that enjoyed a high reputation.

Resettling in the capital city was a journey from poverty to abject poverty. To house his family, Barnett secured a room at the back of a rag and bone shop in Cable Street, situated on the southern border of the Jewish Quarter near the East London docks. The owner of the shop lived with his family in the loft above, which was accessed through the Rosenberg's accommodation. There was a railway line immediately behind the property and both families shared a single toilet together with the various sorters and rubbish collectors who came to dispose of their pickings. Outside there were merchant seamen and stevedores, beggars and drunkards, prostitutes plied their trade and the street was infested with rats. The overwhelming squalor was redeemed only by the dignity and rhythms of the Jewish way of life, the sanctification of 'the home', the dietary laws, the study of the Torah, the sequence of religious festivals and the weekly celebration of the Sabbath, "coming in like a bride".

To make matters worse the Free School was oversubscribed and Isaac had to be sent to the local Board School close to Cable Street. The absorption and socialisation of growing numbers of immigrant children was a formidable task. In London the School Board had adopted an enlightened policy of making Jewish Religious Education available within State Schools. Jewish teachers were recruited, who, in addition to teaching the general curriculum, were able to give religious instruction after regular hours. Absence from school on religious holidays was permitted and in winter pupils were allowed home early on Friday afternoons in time for the arrival of the Sabbath. In this way a pluralistic agenda of Anglicisation combined with respect for Judaism was promoted. Nothing could have demonstrated the difference between Britain and Russia more cogently.

But where minorities are embedded in a dominant culture, freedom not force is the greater catalyst to integration. Unlike his father, Isaac did not take to Hebrew studies, nor was he inspired by the practice of Orthodox Judaism. He played truant from lessons (for which he was caned by his Jewish teachers) and scarcely advanced beyond his Aleph-Bet in the study of the ancient language – necessary for participation in synagogue services. According to his sister, Annie, he recited English poems rather than Hebrew Grace, before, after (and between) meals. It was the history of his People as recounted in the Authorised version of the Old Testament, and Lord Byron's 'Hebrew Melodies', that fired his imagination. Here the plaintive voice of Israel could be heard filtered through the lines of a radical English aristocrat, as in his poem 'Oh! Weep for Those':

> Oh! weep for those that wept by Babel's stream,
> Whose shrines are desolate, whose land a dream;
> Weep for the harp of Judah's broken shell;
> Mourn—where their God hath dwelt, the godless dwell!
>
> And where shall Israel lave her bleeding feet?
> And when shall Zion's songs again be sweet?
> And Judah's melody once more rejoice
> The hearts that leap'd before its heavenly voice?
>
> Tribes of the wandering foot and weary breast,
> How shall ye flee away and be at rest!
> The wild-dove hath her nest, the fox his cave,
> Mankind their country—Israel but the grave!

The kindly encouragement to his artistic interests given by Mr. Usherwood, the Gentile headmaster of Baker Street School, was another important factor in young Isaac's development. By the age of nine the contours of his character were beginning to emerge. He was a frail, serious boy, more interested in reading, drawing and just 'thinking', than running around in the playground during school break; his draughtsmanship was surprisingly accomplished for one so young. He chalked portraits on the pavement outside his house that elicited the astonished admiration of passers-by and sketched on scraps of paper whenever he could. Usherwood soon became aware of his tendency to do this during lessons, but instead of meting out punishment, he indulged Isaac by supplying him with materials and allowing him the privilege of leaving class to work privately in the headmaster's study. In 1902, Usherwood managed to arrange day-release for Isaac to attend the Stepney Green Crafts School once a week, where he learnt art metalwork and was able to mix with other boys and girls who shared his attraction to the arts.

In a letter written in 1920 to the poet Laurence Binyon, Morley Dainow, the librarian in the Public Library at Whitechapel during Rosenberg's childhood, recalls being approached by his sister, Minnie, for help with her younger brother. The letter suggests that his first poem may have been written considerably earlier than hitherto thought:

> A fragile Jewish boy was brought to me by this lady. This boy was Isaac Rosenberg. I took young Rosenberg for walks, and discovered him to be perfectly convinced that his vocation in life was that of a Poet and a Painter. He was then, I believe, between the ages of 10 and 12 years. I enjoyed being with the boy and was much impressed both by his confidence and his sensitivity. In return for my time and interest he sent me 'David's Harp'.

Around the same time Isaac's mother effected an introduction to the young painter, John Amshewitz, which was also fruitful in extending the network of his mentors. Hacha sold her fine embroidery to wealthy Jewish women in North West London and Amshewitz, eight years older than Isaac, already a student at the Royal Academy, was the son of one of her customers. Isaac's prickly emotions betrayed themselves at their first meeting – "I advised him as best I could and awkwardly purchased a drawing with a poem attached for half a crown whereat he burst into tears and rushed from my presence," Amshewitz recalled. It isn't clear whether Isaac felt hurtfully patronised or overwhelmed by the older boy's kindly interest, but Amshewitz later judged him to be a "strange mixture of extreme modesty and assertiveness". Despite this he became convinced that Rosenberg had "a soul far above the ordinary both as an artist and a poet". Over the ensuing years Isaac became a regular visitor in the Amshewitz household. It was in Amshewitz's Hampstead studio that he met the established painters, Solomon J. Solomon and Frank Emanuel, and the middle-aged schoolmistress, Miss Winifreda Seaton, who was to become his confidante.

Isaac's family could not afford to keep him at school beyond the minimum leaving age of fourteen, which he attained in the spring of 1904. Bearing in mind her son's talents, Hacha, on Amshewitz's advice, found what seemed to be a suitable apprenticeship for him in the large engraving firm of Carl Hentschel & Co that produced illustrations for newspapers, periodicals and books. Hentschel, himself the son of Polish immigrants, had set up his business in 1887. It was a progressive enterprise that adopted new technologies, electric lights, telephones, and modern business methods and rapidly expanded. By the end of the century it was turning out more than 60,000 blocks per year from its three 'factories' based in Fleet Street. It was here that Isaac was to spend the next five years. He hated every minute of it, writing a misanthropic early draft to the final stanza of his poem, 'Fleet Street':

> The stony buildings blankly stare
> While murder's being done within
> While man returns his fellow's glare
> The secrets of his soul to miss.
> And each man's heart is foul with lust
> Of women, or the blind gold dust.

And in a letter to Winifreda Seaton, dated 1910:

> It is horrible to think that all these hours, when my days are full of vigour and my hands and soul craving for self-expression, I am bound, chained to this fiendish mangling-machine, without hope and almost desire of deliverance, and the days of youth go by.

Albeit he considered himself a wage slave, the money earned was a welcome contribution to the family income. In addition it enabled him to enrol for evening classes in the Art School at Birkbeck College, which he attended for nearly two years between 1907 and 1908. Under the tutelage of Miss Alice Wright, Rosenberg carried off prizes for a head study in charcoal, several figure drawings, and for a nude in oils. She and her sister shared a passion for poems with her young student, introduced him to the work of Shelley and Blake and like Miss Seaton, developed a friendship that was to continue for years after his time at Birkbeck came to an end.

There was also the Whitechapel Library, otherwise known as the 'University of the Ghetto'. Founded in 1892 and open till 10.00pm every day of the week, its warm and well-lit reading rooms were packed with local people intent on improving themselves.

It was here, sometime in 1907 that Isaac's attempt to sketch the head of another young artist, David Bomberg, led to their meeting and subsequent friendship. Bomberg's reciprocal drawing of Isaac, 'Head of a Poet', would later win the Henry Tonks prize at the Slade School of Art. The two bergs were born within ten days of each other and shared a similar background, but their physical and mental attributes were as different as Hamlet and Hercules. Where Rosenberg, barely five foot two inches, was lean, brooding and shy, Bomberg was stocky and extroverted. His brother, a professional boxer, had taught him how to defend himself. Together the two young men stalked the Library, which like all universities was not just a place of learning. Seen through the eyes of Sonia Cohen, a pretty young seamstress seeking to extricate herself from a dressmaker's sweatshop, they were a couple of poseurs with considerable panache:

> Both wore large-brimmed black hats and neither had the bow or tie usual with this particular headgear. In fact the taller of the two wore an apple-green or sometimes yellow tie which invariably had a red stone pinned onto it; and his companion, he of the slow upturned smile, favoured pink ties. This last mentioned young man once had a whole neck cloth of pink.
>
> The notice 'Silence please' was not for them, at least not for the young man who favoured yellow and apple-green ties. He discussed this one and that among us, while his friend who seldom initiated conversation, smiled or listened with his head lowered and tucked down inwards as if he wished to prevent what he had in his head escaping. At last they sat. And after further scrutiny of the figures before them, each lifted a pencil or crayon and, having levelled it against his nose or contracted eye muscles, first one young man and then the other lowered a right hand and swished it in curves, verticals and diagonals across large sheets of paper they had brought with them.

Isaac inherited his father's intellectual interests and lack of enthusiasm for the humdrum routines of a regular job. It seems he could not wait for the official termination of his apprenticeship. In 1911 as the time drew near, he must have engaged in more and more day-dreaming, eventually re-enacting his father's experience as a trainee tailor, he managed to get himself sacked for inattentiveness. An event which he at first welcomed with a burst of enthusiasm, writing to Miss Seaton, "Congratulate me! I've cleared out of the shop – I hope for good and all", and as the realities struck home very soon came to regret, " ... All one's thoughts seem to revolve round to one point – death. It is horrible, especially at night, 'in the silence of the midnight'; it seems to clutch at your thought – you can't breathe. Oh, I think, work, work, any work, only to stop one thinking". In desperation, hoping to be reinstated, he once again sought the help of Israel Zangwill, who on August 22nd wrote to his friend Hentschel:

> If you recognise the enclosed pencil-sketch it will be a proof of the artistic powers of the sketcher – a young man who claims to have been apprenticed to you for five years and then dismissed 'for slackness' – yours, I presume, not his own.

> This Isaac Rosenberg of 159, Oxford Street, Mile End, E. now finds it difficult to get work and has people dependent on him. He has sent me a batch of compositions in prose and verse, besides his sketch, all showing artistic faculty, so that he ought to be more valuable in your work than the average apprentice.

Hentschel's mind was not to be changed.

3

Art Student

Art is as it were another planet ...

I.R.

If the Library was Whitechapel's university, the local streets were its campus. For young East Enders with little money to spend they provided a cheap and relatively safe place for night time socialising. It was here on the 2nd January, 1911 that the disgruntled earthbound apprentice, Isaac Rosenberg, who longed to escape to the planet of art and literature, first made contact with a group of fellow cultural cosmonauts – Simon Weinstein (later Winsten), Joseph Lefkowitz (later Leftwich) and John Rodker. All were aspiring authors. Winsten was to become the biographer of George Bernard Shaw, Leftwich an anthologist of Hebrew and Yiddish translations and Rodker a novelist, translator, modernist poet and publisher. In 1919 he founded the short-lived Ovid Press which published T.S. Eliot and Ezra Pound. Later he published James Joyce and established the Imago Publishing Company that brought out the complete works of Sigmund Freud.

Leftwich's diary gives a graphic account of the meeting. Rosenberg pulled out a bundle of odd scraps of paper from his pocket and read his poems under a lamppost. The others were impressed. They recognised his work as "real" poetry. Winsten was "awed", Rodker found his work "remarkable" and Leftwich rated him "a genius". Yet he appeared self-absorbed, his demeanour awkward and unattractive, his voice stuttering and monotonous, and his capacity for friendship doubtful. Rosenberg in person belied Rosenberg on paper. Nonetheless he was invited into their circle. With the addition of the artists Bomberg, Mark Gertler and Clara Birnberg, and Sonia Cohen (who later became a dancer and actress), it formed the nucleus of the 'Whitechapel Group'. It was really just a set of young idealistic friends who shared a common background and commitment to the arts.

Bomberg, Rosenberg and Rodker also shared a common attraction to Sonia Cohen. Taking advantage of his friend's reticence, Bomberg had Isaac woo Sonia with poems, playing Cyrano to his own Christian. One evening at the Library, he slipped a poem across the table and placed it on the book that Sonia was reading:

Lady, you are my God—
Lady, you are my heaven.

If I am your God
Labour for your heaven.

Lady you are my God,
And shall not love win heaven?

If love made me God
Deeds must win my heaven.

If my love made you God,
What more can I for heaven?

Sonia was impressed, but not with the poem's invitation to "deeds". She was a sexual naïf but sophisticated enough to recognise the true author of the hyperbole. She soon preferred Rosenberg's high-minded romanticism to Bomberg's clumsy attempts at seduction, which were "horrible". In any event she wasn't physically attracted to small men. Still she must have enjoyed her role as Rosenberg's muse. They went for long walks together, talked compulsively, visited art galleries and according to Sonia kissed (once) in Kensington Gardens. Was it 'The Key Of The Gates Of Heaven'?

A word leapt sharp from my tongue,
Could a golden key do more
Than open the golden door
For the rush of the golden song?
She spoke, and the spell of her speech—
The chain of the heart linked song—
Was on me swift and strong,
And Heaven was in my reach.

A word was the key thereof;
And my thought was the hand that turned.
And words that throbbed and burned,
Sweet birds from the shine of love,
Flew clear 'tween the rosebud gate
That was parted beneath and above,
And a chain of music wove
More strong than the hand of fate.

No it was not. In her mind the relationship was essentially platonic. Rosenberg's unrequited physical passion overflowed into voluptuous verse:

> Like some fair subtle poison is the cold white beauty you shed;
> Pale flower of the garden I walk in, your scent is an amorous net
> To lure my thoughts and pulses, by your useless phantom led
> By misty hours and ruins with insatiate longing wet.
>
> To lure my soul with the beauty of some enthralling sin.
> To starve my body to hunger for the mystic rapture there.
> O cruel; flesh and spirit your robe's soft stir sucks in,
> And your cold unseeing glances, and the fantasies of your hair.
>
> And in the shining hollow of your dream-enhaunted throat
> My mournful thoughts now wander and build desire a nest,
> But no tender thoughts to crown the fiery dreams that float
> Around those sinuous rhythms and dim languors of your breast.

'Like some fair subtle poison' (1912)

It was the youngster, Rodker, only sixteen when he first met Rosenberg and unsympathetically characterised by Leftwich as "tall and thin like a garden-hose and squirts out a lot of water", who was to win Sonia's heart. He was more handsome than the other two, wore a gold earring and had a "magnetic personality". Two years later, much to the frustration of the thwarted elders, she borrowed a distinctly un-gold ring and moved in with him. The free-thinking couple rented a small room above a stationer, an action on Sonia's part which Bomberg enviously described as "going to live with a long, skinny poet in a slot meter".

Life pans out in unexpected ways. Within a few weeks of having left his apprenticeship, Rosenberg, who now spent his days copying old masters in the National Gallery, was noticed at work on a reproduction of Velásquez's 'Philip IV'. The onlooker was herself a well-established and well-connected painter, Lily Delissa Joseph. She was instantaneously drawn to the young East-Ender, effected an introduction discussing technique, and invited him to dinner shortly afterwards. The chance encounter (though Jean Moorcroft Wilson, Rosenberg's biographer, has suggested it might have been a set up), was all the more remarkable because he had been hoping to put together a portfolio that would induce the Jewish Educational Aid Society to back his enrolment in the Slade School of Art. Unbeknown to Lily, it was her own brother, the artist

Solomon J. Solomon acting as a referee for the Society, who having earlier supported the candidature of Gertler and Bomberg, was instrumental in rejecting Isaac's application.

By the end of the summer he was in a slough of despond. Despite having been offered a small amount of work tutoring Lily's son in art and poetry, his savings had nearly run out, he was unemployed, unpublished and unlucky in love. Leftwich noted in his diary that he spoke in a melancholy and dispirited way about his poems, "He is very disappointed. He seems able to do nothing about his work. No one will give him any real encouragement". Rosenberg contemplated taking a cattle boat to America or leaving for Africa. Just as he reached the depths of despair a message arrived from Lily asking him to call. She had made arrangements together with wealthy friends, Mrs Herbert Cohen and Mrs E.D. Löwy, to fund his studies at the Slade. It was as if he had suddenly acquired three fairy godmothers.

Under the direction of Frederick Brown, who had occupied the chair in practical painting since 1893, the Slade had developed a reputation for high standards of draughtsmanship combined with a forward looking enthusiasm for artistic innovation. Brown had recruited an impressive faculty, including Philip Wilson Steer, Ambrose McEvoy and Henry Tonks, a former surgeon from the Royal Free Hospital, who had transferred the time-honoured technique of 'teaching by humiliation' from the ward round to the life class. Many students felt intimidated by his contemptuous veneer but Rosenberg was full of admiration, writing to Miss Seaton, "You've heard of Professor Tonks – he's one of the teachers. A most remarkable man. He talks wonderfully. So voluble and ready – crammed with ideas – most illuminating and suggestive – and witty".

In autumn 1911 when Rosenberg joined the School, Impressionism was already giving way to Post-Impressionism, and Cubism with its assault on our taken-for-granted perceptions, was a movement about to overwhelm the world of modern art. Its close relative, Futurism, launched in 1909 with a manifesto published by the young Italian poet Filippo Marinetti, went even further in its iconoclastic drive to break with the past; revelling in the triumph of machines over nature, glorifying war as a form of social hygiene, flirting with Mussolini's nascent Fascism and looking forward to a future where the old would be superseded by a new era of speed, technology, misogyny and violence.

All this was loathsome to a man who idealised art as a manifestation of beauty. Rosenberg was essentially conservative in his approach. He did not regard museums as "cemeteries of wasted effort" and respected the achievements of the great painters of the past. Art was a constructive force that would release him spiritually from the squalor into which he had been born, and liberate him temporally with an income from portrait painting. Clearly he identified himself with William Blake, the artisan poet-painter-engraver whose transcendental vision rendered him in Rosenberg's view "the highest artist England has ever had". Modernism in the visual arts was a threatening force moving in the opposite direction. It was essentially destructive. "The only sensation I have ever got from a Futurist picture," he would later write, "is that of a house falling [...] We can never strip ourselves completely from associated ideas; and art, being in its form at least, descriptive, the cubes and abrupt angles call to mind falling bricks."

Rosenberg's previous experience meant that he was exempt from several terms in the Antique Room drawing casts of ancient sculpture. He moved directly to the men's life class located in the cigarette-smoke-filled basement of the Slade. Here he was to spend much of the forthcoming two and a half years, honing his skills with sketches from naked models who adopted a sequence of 'ten-minute' poses, changing position at the ring of a bell. He was a conscientious student attending regularly, even on Saturdays, and winning first-class certificates from Brown and Tonks. But this did not stop Mrs Cohen from feeling dissatisfied with his performance or Rosenberg from feeling unfairly criticised.

Problems in their relationship started in the summer of 1912 when he determined to enter a painting for the Slade Summer Competition. It was a large canvas full of nude figures in a dream-like paradisical atmosphere, entitled *Joy*, and according to the artist painted in "a gorgeous scheme of rose pearl and gold". The work, executed in the Hampstead studio rented on his behalf by Michael Sherbrooke (another benefactor with whom he soon fell out), took about three months to complete. It was accomplished with difficulty because propriety demanded that friends and family who acted as models pose fully clothed. When Mrs Cohen saw the picture, far from encouraging him with praise, she criticised it for being unfinished and chided him with a school-marm's 'Could do better'. Unless he got "into a more healthy style of work', she indicated that she would be unable to help him.

Later in the year, things came to a head when she sent him money for fees that was five shillings short of the necessary sum. Instead of passing it on to the authorities, he hung on to the cheque and wrote her what appeared to be a slapdash letter, pointing out the error and requesting additional funds. In the meantime the Slade had contacted her asking for payment. Stung by receiving this direct communication from the School of Art and offended by the ink smudges in Rosenberg's letter that she interpreted as a sign of disrespect, she considered him both arrogant and ungentlemanly. Patronage rarely comes unadulterated by the expectation of payback, even if it is only the wish for a demonstration of gratitude, and Rosenberg's inward-looking demeanour gave little away. Nor would his pride allow him to receive gifts from someone whom he came to regard as interfering in artistic matters and unappreciative of his efforts. Luckily, by the end of the year when Mrs Cohen wrote saying that she did not wish to help "this case" for longer than one more term, the Jewish Educational Aid Society agreed to take over funding for his future studies, thus releasing both parties from a souring dependency relationship.

Rosenberg's gaucheness was also apparent with his peers. He lacked sensitivity to other's feelings or at least appeared to do so when in face to face contact. He had no skill in social networking. Where Bomberg and Gertler soon made connections with avant-garde circles, Rosenberg pursued his own essentially solitary course. A sad anecdote recounted in Joseph Cohen's 1975 biography, *Journey to the Trenches*, has him at the Café Royal, spouting talk about his poetry to a group of fellow students who become progressively more bored and annoyed. Eventually they all connive to leave. One by one, they find an excuse to go – to the toilet, to the telephone, to the exit – until Rosenberg is left talking to himself, unaware that he has been landed with the bill.

His shyness combined with diminutive size, working-class background and marked East End accent punctuated by a stutter, made him more vulnerable to anti-Semitic bullying. Alvaro Guevara, the Chilean painter, was his chief persecutor, from whom Rosenberg received a regular stream of abuse to which he did not react. Other Jewish students, however, less inhibited about using their fists, were not prepared to tolerate the Chilean's behaviour. Bomberg and Jacob Kramer intervened on Rosenberg's behalf and brought the taunting to an end.

It has been suggested that Rosenberg's development as a painter would have been better served at the Royal Academy with its more traditional approach to art and interest in portraiture. Certainly he did not emerge from the Slade with an entrance ticket into the terrestrial 'World of Art'. In retrospect his contemporaries remembered him more for his interest in poetry than his talent with the paintbrush. Bomberg waggishly characterised him as "the Poet Laureate, less the title and the retaining fee". And Cohen concludes that with its emphasis on clean lines and precise draughtsmanship, "Perhaps the Slade's greatest benefit was to make him a better poet".

4

Budding Poet

Nothing is rarer than good poetry—and nothing more discouraging than the writing of poetry.

I.R.

Rosenberg's twin ambitions to be both a painter and a poet were not mutually exclusive. Apart from William Blake there was also the example of another hero, Dante Gabriel Rossetti, whose reputation had continued to grow during the decades following his death in 1882. Rosenberg thought Rossetti's pen-and-ink drawings were "the cream" of the Pre-Raphaelite Exhibition mounted by the Tate Gallery in winter 1911/12. As for his poems, according to Rosenberg, he "never published anything that wasn't good". Bearing in mind Isaac's suppressed passion for Sonia, it isn't surprising that 'The Song of the Bower', suffused as it is with unfulfilled longing and missed opportunity, was a particular favourite. Its final lines read:

> Peace, peace! such a small lamp illumes, on this highway,
> So dimly so few steps in front of my feet,—
> Yet shows me that her way is parted from my way …
> Out of sight, beyond light, at what goal may we meet?

In fact the lingua franca of poetry during the years leading up to the First World War remained steeped in romanticism. Poets dealt or struggled with 'big' subjects, the meaning of life and death, the mysteries of the universe, the transcendental nature of mind, unrequited love and inexpressible desire. They exalted 'nature' and bemoaned the evils of 'the city'. There was a conventional quasi-Biblical archaic language. To be poetic was to self-consciously fix the syllable 'en' to the beginning or end of a verb; to use words like 'O' and 'Ye', 'Thee' and 'Thou', 'doth' and 'Lo'; to invert the order of adjective and noun, verb and adverb. It was to select words from a special lexicon set aside from every day speech, 'mould' instead of earth, 'illume' in place of light up. And it was to make frequent reference to heavenly bodies, precious metals, light and dark, lamps, mirrors, hearts, souls, spirits and God (even if the author was an unbeliever). As the American poet, Ezra Pound, commented: "The common verse in Britain from 1890 [the year of Rosenberg's birth] was a horrible agglomerate compost, not minted, most of it not even baked, all legato, a doughy mess of third-hand Keats, Wordsworth, heaven knows what, fourth-hand Elizabethan sonority blunted, half-melted, lumpy".

Laurence Binyon's work is a good example of the kind of poetry being written in Rosenberg's time. Binyon, famous now for penning the lines:

> They shall grow not old, as we that are left grow old:
> Age shall not weary them, nor the years condemn.
>
> At the going down of the sun and in the morning,
> We will remember them.

was the son of a Quaker minister. Educated at St Paul's School, he went on to study Classics at Trinity College, Oxford and worked in the British Museum's Department of Prints and Drawings. Separated from Rosenberg by more than twenty years in age, by education, by religion and by social class, it seems unlikely that their paths would have crossed. But Rosenberg was never slow to make contact with recognised literary figures in order to seek feedback on his work and help in promoting it. His inhibitions in company didn't apply to the written word. His letters reveal a more personable character than do descriptions of his behaviour, and he was obviously more confident in correspondence than conversation.

In the Spring of 1912, despite having been recently advised by Zangwill's cousin, Dr David Eder (an early psychoanalyst, physician and writer), in the nicest possible terms, "not to think of publishing yet awhile", and despite knowing "that he was right", Rosenberg decided that the criticism did not apply to his latest poems and promptly sent them off to Binyon. The response that came, almost by return of post, must have been more enthusiastic than he could possibly have imagined. Binyon was impressed and wanted to arrange a meeting at the British Museum. Recording his reactions to the encounter at a later date, he found that Rosenberg had an "earnest, transparent sincerity" about him, and was struck by "how strangely little of second-hand (in one of his age) there was in his opinions, how fresh a mind he brought to what he saw and read". He also noted an "unusual mixture of self-reliance and modesty". Binyon took a serious interest in Rosenberg's work, exchanging poems with him, giving advice and maintaining a correspondence that lasted at least until 1917. After the war he wrote an introductory memoir to the 1922 First Edition of *Poems by Isaac Rosenberg*, edited by Gordon Bottomley.

One has only to compare Binyon's poem 'The Mirror', probably sent to Rosenberg some time in 1912, who found the opening stanzas especially appealing for "the rapture they rise into":

> Where is all the beauty that hath been?
> Where the bloom?
> Dust on boundless wind? Grass dropt into fire?
> Shall earth boast at last of all her teeming womb,
> all that suffered, all that triumphed to inspire
> life in perfect mould and speech, the proud mind's lamp serene—
> nothing? Space be starry in tremendous choir—
> for whom?
>
> In this deserted chamber, as the evening falls,
> silent curtains move no fold;
> long has ebbed the floor's pale gold;
> shadows deepen down the silent walls.
> The air is mute as dreams beneath a sleeper's face,
> distant, undivined;
> but every hovering shadow seems to hold
> want untold.
> The look of things forsaken, each in its own place,
> memories without home in any mind,
> idle, rich neglect and perfume old—
> over these the glimmer of the twilight fades;
> infinite human solitude invades
> forms relinquished, hues resigned.

with the first stanza of Rosenberg's 'Night and Day':

> When the night is warm with wings
> Invisible, articulate,
> Only the wind sings
> To our mortal ears of fault.
> And the steadfast eyes of fate
> Gleam from Heaven's brooding vault,
> Through dull corporeal bars
> We drink in the proud stars.
> These, my earth-sundered fantasy
> On pillared heights of thought doth see
> In the dark heaven as golden pendulous birds,

> Whose tremulous wings the wind translates to words,
> From the thrilled heaven which is their rapturous nest.
> Still, though they sleep not, thoughtful to illume,
> They are not silent, only our sundering gloom
> Makes their songs dumb to us—a tragic jest.

to see that the two poets were writing in the same genre, using a similar stock of words and giving expression to a shared view of the human condition. Man was alone in the Universe. But Rosenberg's protagonist is redeemed when day breaks. He wakes and according to the poem's prefatory Argument "feels endowed with a larger capacity to feel and enjoy things, and knows that by having communed with the stars, his soul has exalted itself".

Buoyed up by Binyon's attention and having had little success in getting his work published in magazines let alone book form, Rosenberg decided to have a pamphlet printed himself. He selected ten items including the sonnet he had written 'To J. H. Amschewitz', 'Aspiration', 'Spiritual Isolation', 'O! In a World of Men and Women', and a group of love poems – 'Heart's first Word', 'When I went Forth', 'In November', 'Lady you are my God', and 'Tess', together with all three hundred and twenty-one lines of 'Night and Day' as the title poem. His friend Reuben (otherwise known as 'Crazy') Cohen, who worked for the East End printer, Israel Narodiczky, undertook the work. Narodiczky, who had a soft spot for 'alternative' causes, agreed to produce fifty copies of a twenty-four page pamphlet for the reduced sum of £2, which Rosenberg persuaded Mrs Cohen to advance on the understanding that he would repay her from the proceeds of sales. It was a sanguine promise. Then, as now, the chances of an unknown poet selling work were negligible. Unsurprisingly, by the end of the summer despite the best efforts of Leftwich, who stood outside Toynbee Hall touting for custom, all copies had been given away or sent to editors and none had been sold. Rosenberg assured Mrs Cohen that he was going to sell a drawing for £4 which would provide money to discharge the loan.

On top of everything else his health was beginning to deteriorate. In December 1912 he needed the services of an ophthalmologist and in early 1913, after returning to live with his parents now at 87 Dempsey Street, Stepney, he developed a bad cough that lingered for a couple of months. It wasn't a serious chest complaint, but his doctor advised fresh air and a trip away from London. Travelling together with Bomberg, the two young men visited the Isle of Wight where they were able to stay in accommodation owned by Mrs Haydon, a longstanding customer of Rosenberg's father. It was situated in Southdown near the island's military fortifications, which they naively decided would make a good subject for painting. However the local police thought differently and arrested them on suspicion of spying. They were only released after the landlady was able to vouch for their character, or so the story goes!

Nineteen-thirteen wasn't good for Rosenberg. His artistic output was meagre and his mental state was, on the whole, despondent. But in November of that year a meeting with Edward Marsh at the Café Royal engineered by Gertler, was to have far-reaching consequences. Of a similar age to Binyon and also educated in the Classics, Marsh was a civil servant working as Private Secretary to Winston Churchill, then First Lord of the Admiralty. He mixed in high society. His great-grandfather, Sir Spencer Perceval, bore the dubious distinction of having been the only British Prime Minister to be assassinated. As a result parliament had voted a sum of £50,000 to be settled on his progeny. Marsh used his share of the inheritance, what he called "murder money", together with a legacy from a "mad" aunt, to patronise the arts.

In particular he had gathered around him a retinue of young men, including Gertler, Bomberg, and the poets, Rupert Brooke and Siegfried Sassoon. No doubt he was a suppressed homosexual at a time when homoerotic acts were a criminal offence. His biographer, Christopher Hassall, suggests implausibly that Marsh's sexual orientation "devotion characteristically feminine in its tenderness", was somehow related to impotence deriving from the complications of mumps in teenage years. Marsh took an immediate shine to Rosenberg, admitting him into his circle of protégés and launching a fatherly friendship that would continue to the end of his life. He invited him to dine at his club, corresponded with him regularly, bought paintings and drawings, read his poetry and provided criticism. During 1915 he funded the self-publication of Rosenberg's second volume of poems, *Youth*, in return for which the poet-painter gave him three nude studies. In addition he invited Rosenberg to contribute to an anthology of *Georgian Drawings* (that was never actually published), and included an extract from his verse play 'Moses', in the third of his five popular *Georgian Anthologies*, published in 1917. Marsh helped Rosenberg in other ways; he introduced him to the poets, Lascelles Abercrombie and Gordon Bottomley, and to the work of James Elroy Flecker. And he provided administrative advice and assistance when necessary in Rosenberg's affairs. But Marsh was very much a figure of the establishment whose taste in poetry inclined toward traditional forms at a time when the modernist revolution was about to sweep them away. Albeit he tried to curb Rosenberg's more extravagant excursions into vagueness, he probably acted as a break on his poetic development.

In a lecture entitled 'Romanticism and Classicism', T.E Hulme, whom Rosenberg met on the same evening he was introduced to Marsh, had already codified the principles that were to guide the forthcoming cultural upheaval in poetry. For Hulme, "romanticism" in verse was predicated on Jean Jacques Rousseau's notion of man as a reservoir of infinite possibility. Romantic poets were always striving to express the inexpressible and forever falling into a mire of meaningless evocation. Their poetry was gloomy because their aspirations could never be fulfilled. "Classical" verse, on the other hand, happily accepted man's limitations, it had its feet on the ground, it sought only to describe the world, not to go beyond it. Classical poetry focused on the concrete, was dry, hard, unsentimental, sparse. It never flew away "into the circumambient gas". Rosenberg, almost against his own will, would be propelled in this direction. He could have done with the intellectual companionship available from this philosopher-poet. However Hulme, only seven years older than Rosenberg, was no father-figure and no potential patron – a relationship never developed.

Hulme's thinking, however, which underpinned the poetic philosophy of the developing 'Imagists', was certainly familiar to Rosenberg by the time he met Marsh. The term "Imagistes" (later spelt without the e) had been coined by Ezra Pound the previous year, to describe the work of his ex-fiancée, Hilda Doolitle (H.D.) and the young poet, Richard Aldington. Another member of the group, F.S. Flint, contributed explanatory notes to the March 1913 edition of *Poetry*, edited by Harriet Monroe. He expounded three rules that characterised the movement:

1. Direct treatment of the 'thing' whether subjective or objective.
2. To use absolutely no word that did not contribute to presentation.
3. As regarding rhythm: to compose in sequence of the musical phrase not in sequence of a metronome.

Miss Seaton must have drawn Rosenberg's attention to Flint's work, which he reacted to with enjoyment but muted enthusiasm, writing to her:

> I suppose Flint's poems gave me pleasure because of their newness to me. They don't seem to be ambitious, they seem to me just experiments in versification … Dr Eder told me he was very young, about 22 [the same age as Rosenberg]; and I expect he'll do something yet.

Clearly Rosenberg was still in thrall to the masters of the past, as represented by Rossetti, and less than impressed with his contemporaries, who were set on forging a radically new poetics for the twentieth century.

Isaac's student days came to an end in the spring of 1914. It was not only that the money for fees had run out, but also that Professor Brown had failed to recommend to the JEAS that he complete the course. It may be no coincidence that Bomberg had been kicked out the previous year because his views were considered a "disturbing influence" on other students. In any event Rosenberg's commitment to poetry had become paramount. Hence the title of Bomberg's drawing 'Head of a Poet' and the alteration of Rosenberg's poem originally entitled 'The Artist' and subsequently changed to 'The Poet'. Perhaps this shift in priorities combined with a melancholic disposition and diminished output, to influence Brown's decision.

If he had been disinclined to take the kind of work available to a working-class Jewish East Ender before he entered the Slade, he was now thoroughly unsuited for life as a tailor or furrier. He hated dependency, especially upon his impecunious family, yet there was no realistic prospect of him earning money from poetry and little chance of sufficient income from painting. In the absence of employment as a teacher, he was going to need patronage for the foreseeable future.

5

Cape Town

Across the bay the piled up mountains of Africa look lovely and dangerous. It makes one think of savagery and earthquakes—the elemental lawlessness.

I.R.

No longer a student, lacking employment, and having been advised by his doctor to live in the country, Rosenberg once again began to dream of getting away from it all. This time, however, an opportunity presented itself. His sister, Minnie, had married a South African post-office clerk, Wolf Horvitch, the previous year. The couple had settled in 'District Six', an area of Cape Town not unlike the East End of London with a large population of Lithuanian Jewish émigrés. Two of Rosenberg's uncles also lived in the city, and there were cousins. When Minnie heard of Isaac's ill health she prevailed upon him to join them. He would be able to stay with them until he found work to support himself, he might even work on a farm for a year or two, Rosenberg fancifully wrote to Marsh. In addition he would have access to cheap models and be able to paint "real" things and escape the need to "do Cubism".

Paradoxically, it was just at this moment that five of his paintings had been included in an exhibition mounted at the Whitechapel Art Gallery, entitled *Twentieth Century Art: A Review of Modern Movements*. Since Rosenberg's work was about as far as you could get from breaking new ground, it isn't surprising that it was badly reviewed. But by the time the exhibition opened he had already embarked for Africa on a Union Castle steamship, the steerage fare money of £12 having been provided once again by a benevolent JEAS. Rosenberg wasn't worried about missing London; it was a city that instilled a feeling of selfishness and alienation in its inhabitants. According to his biographer, Joseph Cohen, Rosenberg was engaged in a relationship with a young music teacher, Annetta Raphael, to whom he had lost his virginity, but this obviously wasn't enough to hold him back. "I hardly know anybody whom I would regret leaving," he wrote to Miss Seaton, but he understood his own character too, adding "but whether it is that my nature distrusts people, or is intolerant, or whether my pride or my backwardness cools people, I have always been alone".

One should be circumspect in inferring biographical data from works of art, poems are not factual reports; however 'Sacred, Voluptuous Hollows Deep' doesn't read like a work of pure imagination. Written sometime during the period under discussion, there is nothing "cool" about it. The second stanza reproduced below, shows Rosenberg's full-blooded capacity for passionate human contact, despite his sense of existential isolation:

> Warm, fleshly chambers of delights,
> Whose lamps are we, our days and nights.
> Where our thoughts nestle, our lithe limbs
> Frenzied exult till vision swims
> In fierce delicious agonies;
> And the crushed life bruised through and through,
> Ebbs out, trophy no spirit slew,
> While molten sweetest pains enmesh
> The life sucked by dissolving flesh.

Cohen thinks it was inspired by Annetta, but Jean Moorcroft Wilson, Rosenberg's most recent biographer, believes it was written later in the year and derived from an affair with the South African actress, Margueretha Van Hulsteyn.

Equipped with a letter of introduction written by Marsh to Sir Herbert Stanley, a member of the government, Rosenberg arrived in South Africa at the end of June. He took up residence in the crowded accommodation of his heavily pregnant sister. Early impressions sent back to England reveal a disappointed d'haut en bas voice, utterly at odds with his cockney background. "Think of me, a creature of the most exquisite civilisation, planted in this barbarous land," he wrote to Marsh. The eyes and ears of the local population were clogged up with "gold dust, diamond dust, stocks and shares and heaven knows what other flinty muck", yet "nobody seemed to have money", by which he must have meant that he hadn't yet found a wealthy patron. Nonetheless, within a short time, he had developed a characteristic 'double life' – living in straitened circumstances whilst hobnobbing with the rich and rare of the Capetonian art world.

Ruth Alexander, wife of Morris, a member of the South African Legislative Assembly, was a young Anglo-Jewish migrant who had set up a salon for writers, artists and poets at her home. She took Rosenberg under her wing, admitting him into her network of friends. It was through Ruth and her contacts that Rosenberg met the radical feminist, Betty Molteno, her partner

Alice Greene (aunt of Graham Greene) and later, when he returned to London, the political activist, Olive Schreiner. He may even have encountered Gandhi at her house. He also met and became friendly with the far-from-radical artist, Edward Roworth (notorious in future times for having endorsed Hitler's condemnation of 'Degenerate Art'). He had trained at the Slade under Tonks in an older generation of students. Over six and a half feet, Roworth's giant presented a comic appearance next to Rosenberg's dwarf when the two were walking together. In typical self-deprecating style Rosenberg quipped, "I suppose I haven't quarrelled with Roworth because he never hears what I say, he's so tall".

Roworth introduced Rosenberg to the beautiful bohemian actress, Margueretha (Scrappy) Van Hulsteyn. Daughter of Sir Willem and Lady Van Hulsteyn, she was keen on poetry, four years younger than Rosenberg but already married and divorced from J.G Strijdom, who was to become South Africa's fifth Prime Minister. Known locally as an 'enfant terrible', she had adopted the stage name of Marda Vanne. Whether or not Rosenberg had an affair with her, he certainly captured her image in pencil and presented her with a fair copy of one of his poems written before they met:

> If you are fire and I am fire,
> Who blows the flames apart
> So that desire eludes desire
> Around one central heart?
>
> A single root and separate bough,
> And what blind hands between
> That make our longing's mutual glow
> As if it had not been?

He may have been barking up the wrong tree. In later life she lived for many years with the British actress Gwen Ffrangçon-Davies. When questioned about her relationship with Rosenberg, she claimed she couldn't even remember him. Yet the prodigious output of poems and paintings during the eight months he stayed in South Africa indicates an emotional stirring on Rosenberg's part for which she was the most likely inspiration.

Marda's friend Madge Cook, already an established painter in Cape Town with a studio of her own, and her mother Agnes, did become committed fans of the young Englishman, seeing him as a torch-bearer for progressive ideas. If Rosenberg was old hat in London he was new-fashioned in the Southern Hemisphere. Both of them regarded him as an unsung genius. Agnes, who claimed descent from a Scottish earl, hosted monthly At-Homes to which she invited "lonely foreigners". She was also the editor of a magazine, *South African Women in Council*, and soon arranged to publish two of Rosenberg's poems as well as the lectures on art he had given to the town's Drawing Club.

Scarcely a month after his arrival in Cape Town, August 4th, saw the outbreak of the First World War. The Union of South Africa had been a British Dominion since its creation four years earlier and unhesitatingly joined the allies. It sent forces to German South West Africa (now Namibia). Martial law was declared on 14th October and a rebellion of recalcitrant Boers who wished to side with Germany was put down by government forces in ten days. But Rosenberg seemed superficially unperturbed by all this. To him the war was a distant European affair. It was awful but perhaps it would be over quickly; nobody could have known the extent of the horrors in store. "By the time you get this," he wrote to Marsh, "Europe will have just stepped into its bath of blood. I will be waiting with beautiful drying towels of painted canvas, and precious ointments to smear and heal the soul; and lovely music and poems". Hindsight lends his almost blithe words a poignant irony.

Whether at a deeper level the knowledge of war was affecting Rosenberg, whether it was his love life in South Africa, the experience of maternal fury in his family or the ingrained working of Kabbalistic Jewish legend, probably all four; there is no doubt that the image of a malign, seductive, female God, a motif that would run through much of his subsequent work, appeared with renewed imaginative force at this time. Rosenberg complained to Marsh that he got no privacy and couldn't write or even think – yet he enclosed a number of poems including a draft of his latest effort 'The Female God':

> We curl into your eyes.
> They drink our fires and have never drained.
> In the fierce forest of your hair
> Our desires beat blindly for their treasure.
>
> In your eyes' soundless pit
> Far down, glimmer our souls.
> And your hair like massive forest trees
> Shadows our pulses, overtired and dumb.
>
> Like a candle lost in an electric glare
> Our spirits tread your eyes' infinities.
> In the wrecking waves of your tumultuous locks.
> Do you not hear the moaning of our pulses?

Queen! Goddess! animal!
In sleep do your dreams battle with our souls?
When your hair is spread like a lover on the pillow,
Do not our jealous pulses wake between?

You have dethroned the ancient God.
You have usurped his Sabbath, his common days,
Yea! every moment is delivered to you.
Our Temple! our Eternal! our one God!

Our souls have passed into your eyes
Our days into your hair.
And you, our rose-deaf prison are very pleased with the
  world.
Your world.

It is also possible to read the presence of Lilith, Adam's mythological first demonic wife, intent on using her female powers to destabilise man's inner and outer worlds, into Rosenberg's more explicit response to the opening of hostilities 'On Receiving News of the War':

Snow is a strange white word;
No ice or frost
Have asked of bud or bird
For Winter's cost.

Yet ice and frost and snow
From earth to sky
This Summer land doth know,
No man knows why.

In all men's hearts it is.
Some spirit old
Hath turned with malign kiss
Our lives to mould.

Red fangs have torn His face.
God's blood is shed.
He mourns from His lone place
His children dead.

O! ancient crimson curse!
Corrode, consume.
Give back this universe
Its pristine bloom.

The destructive force is in "all men's hearts", but it has been put there by "some spirit old" through the agency of a "malign kiss". The imagery – incongruous ice, frost and snow in a hot land, is redolent of Rosenberg's earlier poem, 'Midsummer Frost', in which we find the lines, "How, like a sad thought buried in light words, / Winter, an alien presence, is ambushed here". This may be a clue to his state of mind and go some way to explaining the contrast between the apparently flippant dismissal of war in his correspondence with Marsh and his underlying mood. Nonetheless the poem ends on a note that seems alien. It seems to glorify war in the manner of the 'Futurists', invoking the "ancient crimson curse" as an instrument that will through its corrosive power ultimately result in a renewal of life. One wonders if the poet got carried away with his own rhetoric.

The two poems that Agnes Cook selected for publication in the December issue of *South African Women in Council*, 'Beauty' (II), a hymn to some kind of "original innocence" written in rhyming couplets, and 'The Dead Heroes', an astonishing anthem for a man who would later disclaim all patriotic convictions, are of poor quality, a far cry from the above. Yet they so impressed Mrs Cook's friend Betty Molteno that she invited the author to spend some time with her in Sandown House, located in the affluent and beautiful suburb of Rondebosch. She even proposed to rent a room for him in the neighbouring area of Bishop's Court, a generous offer that Rosenberg, despite his constant complaints of lack of peace and quiet for work, found himself unable to accept.

Although he enjoyed his stay with Miss Molteno, who was daughter to Sir John Molteno (first Prime Minister of the Cape after the Union Act) and sister to the Speaker of the Legislative Assembly, it obviously made him acutely aware of the difference in their circumstances. "I'm living like a toff here," he wrote back to his parents, "Early in the morning coffee is brought to me in bed. My shoes (my only pair) are polished so brightly that the world is pleasantly deceived as to the tragedy that polish covers. I don't know whether there are snakes or wild animals in my room, but in the morning when I get up and look at the soles of my shoes, every morning I see another hole". Allowing for Rosenberg's sense of humour, it might nonetheless have been a metaphor revealing his underlying frame of mind.

It seems clear that Rosenberg was a 'difficult' character. The Rev. A.P. Bender, minister of Cape Town's main synagogue at the time, is on record as thinking Rosenberg "a blooming nuisance", a man who "didn't know what he wanted". He had ostensibly gone to South Africa not just for health reasons but also to find work. Yet according to his friend Morris Robinson he sabotaged at least two job opportunities, one of them in a local art school before the interview had even begun. He apparently attended wearing a hat that he refused to remove. When the incensed head teacher threatened to throw him out of the room unless he complied, Rosenberg defiantly told him to "Go to Hell". Similarly when he received a commission to paint an important local business man and Robinson asked when he was going to start, Rosenberg replied "Never". He apparently took exception to the appearance of the man who "looked too prosperous".

By the time Rosenberg wrote to his parents with news of the holiday in Rondebosch at the end of 1914, he had already decided to return home the following March. He had received more recognition in South Africa than ever he had in the larger society of London. He had been welcomed into the close Jewish community of the Cape and taken to the bosom of its high society. He had been provided with work opportunities, delivered lectures on Art, published poems, and possibly had a love affair with Marda Vanne. He had regained his health. Yet he remained disconsolate. The friendships he had forged and the admiration he had generated in some, did not counterbalance his contempt for the small society of Cape Town whose materialism he despised. And a change of environment could not, ultimately, produce a change in his own conflict-ridden inner world. It is unlikely that he came back in order to join up. There is no mention of it in correspondence and it was to be another six months before he made that fateful decision. Jean Moorcroft Wilson thinks he was simply homesick. In any event he set sail for England in February 1915 carrying with him a bundle of paintings, most of which he managed to lose overboard in the shimmering sea of Cape Town harbour!

6

Down-and-Out

You have shown that you are interested in me so I thought you would not mind lending me the 10 shillings to pay as it is so very little and I could easily return it as soon as I get work.

I.R.

Having no means to support himself, Rosenberg took up residence with his family in Dempsey Street. Nothing had changed in the longstanding bitterness between his parents, but the England to which he returned had changed beyond recognition. It was now clear that the war wouldn't be over quickly. Although conscription was not introduced until 1916, the social pressure to volunteer was immense. Over a million allied soldiers had already been killed in France and Belgium. Many of the poets and painters of his generation had enlisted early on, including Siegfried Sassoon. Lord Kitchener's finger pointed at every man between nineteen and thirty-eight years of age from posters all over the country, and young women roamed the streets shaming those not in military uniform, by presenting them with a white feather that indicated cowardice. The practice had become so widespread that on March 1st the Home Secretary was asked in parliament whether he was aware, "that persons employed directly or indirectly in the service of the State are subjected to insolence and provocation at the hands of some advertising young women presenting them with white feathers; and if he will give orders to the police to arrest such persons for acting in a manner likely to create a breach of the peace".

Public interest in the arts had dwindled; indeed they were looked at contemptuously by many, as unproductive and unworthy forms of occupation. Bomberg had been forced to give up painting and start "rubbing down the enamel on second-hand cars" for a living. Gertler was still receiving a regular allowance from Marsh in return for first option on his pictures, but would subsequently break with him over attitudes toward the war, and become a conscientious objector. Leftwich, having been born in Holland, was a 'neutral alien' and thus exempt from military service, Rodker and Winsten would be imprisoned after conscription was introduced. And Rosenberg, British citizen, took up where he had left off, continuing to paint, draw, solicit patronage and send off poems to London editors, but he was not happy.

He executed a fine pencil drawing of his father, a number of portraits including one of himself in a felt hat that now hangs in The National Portrait Gallery, and an accomplished painting of Sonia looking forlorn – not surprisingly as she had separated from Rodker, was in an advanced state of pregnancy, and had been recently evicted from her lodgings. In the spring he sent Marsh poems and in a concession to cubism, a strange charcoal and wash composition entitled 'Hark, Hark, the Lark', portraying six naked figures that seem at once joyful and terrified. He also completed a chalk drawing imbued with erotic tension, 'The First Meeting of Adam and Eve'.

'God Made Blind', written at this time, expresses the complex emotional metabolism operating in Rosenberg's inner world:

> It were a proud God-guiling, to allure
> And flatter, by some cheat of ill, our Fate
> To hold back the perfect crookedness, its hate
> Devised, and keep it poor,
> And ignorant of our joy—
> Masked in a giant wrong of cruel annoy,
> That stands as some bleak hut to frost and night,
> While hidden in bed is warmth and mad delight.
>
> For all Love's heady valour and loved pain
> Towers in our sinews that may not suppress
> (Shut to God's eye) Love's springing eagerness,
> And mind to advance his gain
> Of gleeful secrecy
> Through dolorous clay, which his eternity
> Has pierced, in light that pushes out to meet
> Eternity without us, heaven's heat.
>
> And then, when Love's power hath increased so
> That we must burst or grow to give it room,
> And we can no more cheat our God with gloom,
> We'll cheat Him with our joy.
> For say! what can God do
> To us, to Love, whom we have grown into?
> Love! the poured rays of God's Eternity!
> We are grown God—and shall His self-hate be?

It is a measure of the demand he made on readers that he should think this work easily accessible. "For God's Sake! don't say they're obscure," he wrote to Marsh, "I should think it very clear", explaining the serpentine logic of the poem:

> That we can cheat our malignant fate who has devised a perfect evil for us, by pretending to have as much misery as we can bear, so that it witholds its greater evil, while under that guise of misery there is secret joy. Love – this joy – burns and grows within us trying to push out to that. Eternity without us which is God's heart. Joy-love, grows in time too vast to be hidden from God under the guise of gloom. Then we find another way of cheating God. Now through the very joy itself. For this time we have grown into love, which is the rays of that Eternity of which God is the sun. We have become God Himself. Can God hate and do wrong to Himself?

Rosenberg published 'God Made Blind', together with several new poems and half a dozen reprinted from 'Night and Day' in a second self-generated pamphlet entitled 'Youth'. In return for three life drawings, Marsh covered Narodiczky's costs of £2-10 for printing a hundred copies. Ten were apparently sold, one can only imagine to friends and well-wishers. But Marsh also showed his work to the 'Georgian' poets, Lascelles Abercrombie and Gordon Bottomley, both of whom reacted positively. Abercrombie told Rosenberg that he had the ability "to make the concealed poetic power in words come flashing out" and that "no one who tried to write poetry could help envying some of his writing". And Bottomley would write "There is nothing you cannot do when you have once made firm your hold on the qualities within your reach", encouraging him to tap the Old Testament for stories that he thought underrepresented in English poetry. Rosenberg later gave Bottomley his drawing of Adam and Eve.

Earlier in the year, in response to advances made by the Turks in Southern Russia, Winston Churchill had devised a plan to take Constantinople by forcing an army through the Dardanelles, a heavily-guarded twenty-eight mile strait between Europe and Asiatic Turkey. While being transported to the theatre of operations, Rupert Brooke, Marsh's favourite, developed septicaemia following a mosquito bite. He was transferred to a hospital ship off the Greek island of Skyros, where he died on 23rd April. Marsh was devastated. It must have been especially difficult to bear since as Churchill's Private Secretary, he may have felt involved in sending Brooke to his death. Moreover the campaign turned out to be a disastrous failure. Turkish defences were bolstered by German heavy guns and over 200,000 men were eventually killed. Churchill was blamed for the losses and removed from his job shortly after Brooke's death, adding to Marsh's woes.

In the midst of his grief Rosenberg's concerns took second place. Rosenberg sent his condolences, but attempts to sell Marsh paintings, laced with his own self-pity, began to seem like thoughtless pestering. At the end of the month he wrote Marsh, "Forgive my weak and selfish letter. I should not have disturbed you at all but one gets so bewildered in this terrible struggle". It would be half a year before he wrote to Marsh again. Fortuitously for Rosenberg, it was just at this time that he met Sydney Schiff, a wealthy English Jew with literary interests and connections, who was willing to step into Marsh's shoes.

Among the people to whom Rosenberg sent a copy of 'Youth', plus other manuscripts, were Schiff and Ezra Pound. Schiff replied promptly enclosing ten shillings and saying that he was forwarding the work to the Irish poet, Herbert Trench, for an opinion. He also advised Isaac to show 'Youth' to the critic, Arthur Clutton-Brock. As for his verse drama, 'Moses', Schiff had found it "a little difficult to follow". Pound's response was somewhat different. He sent the poems on to Harriet Monroe in Chicago, editor of the influential magazine, *Poetry*, saying "Don't bother about Rosenberg, send the stuff back to him unless it amuses you", and advised the hopeful poet to join the army! However, when Monroe asked Pound for further advice, he did make a condescending recommendation:

> I think you may as well give this poor devil a show. Yeats called him to my attention last winter, but I have waited. I think you might do half a page review of his book, and that he is worth a page for verse.

He singled out the poem, 'At Night' (reproduced below), as being "good enough" and ended with, "He has something in him, horribly rough but then 'Stepney, East' … we ought to have a real burglar … ma che!!!"

> Crazed shadow from no golden body
> That I can see, embraces me warm;
> All is purple and closed
> Round by night's arm.
>
> A brilliance wings from dark-lit voices,
> Wild lost voices of shadows white.
> See the long houses lean
> To the weird flight.

Star-amorous things that wake at sleep-time
(Because the sun spreads wide like a tree
With no good fruit for them)
Thrill secrecy.

Pale horses ride before the morning
The secret roots of the sun to tread,
With hoofs shod with venom
And ageless dread,

To breathe on burning emerald grasses,
And opalescent dews of the day,
And poison at the core
What smiles may stray.

Pound was particularly impressed with "the sun spreads wide like a tree", but "See the long houses lean / To the weird flight" is, perhaps, equally good. What strikes one in this highly original well-crafted poem, written mainly in unforced quatrains rhyming second and fourth lines, is the distance the poet has travelled since his earlier hackneyed evocation in 'Night and Day'.

The war dragged on, becoming ever closer to the civilian population. In May the *Lusitania*, a Cunard passenger liner on its way from America to the United Kingdom, was sunk by a German U-boat off the coast of Ireland with massive loss of life. Rosenberg tried to write a poem about it. The German High Command also made the decision to bomb the British mainland using airships. The London docklands were a prime target and one fell close to the Rosenbergs' house, burning down a factory and killing several people. Anti-German feeling ran high. Unnaturalised Russians, such as many in Rosenberg's parents' generation, were officially 'friendly aliens', but popular hatred and fear of spies was indiscriminately directed toward anyone with a German-sounding name. In the East End of London shops were attacked, leading some to put up signs explaining their Russian origins. Even the Hanoverian, King George V, would eventually change his name from Saxe-Coburg-Gotha to the English-sounding Windsor. In the midst of this, it is scarcely surprising that Rosenberg and Crazy Cohen's attempt to found a magazine entitled 'The Jewish Standard', in which his South African art lectures featured, folded after the first edition.

Rosenberg grew tired of having to schmooze patrons, writing to Schiff in October that he had decided to pursue "an honest trade", by which he meant "work that I would not be put to all sorts of shifts and diplomatics to dispose of". Desperation had driven him back to the only employer he ever had –

Hentschel – but he now needed to attend evening classes in order to learn the skills involved in preparing blocks for the press. The work would be very unhealthy, bending over strong acids all day, obviously self-destructive for a man with a weak chest; but he thought he could learn enough in two months and prevailed upon Schiff to give him a loan of ten shillings for the fees. Schiff provided the money accompanied by a nostrum for Rosenberg's self-pity, reminding him that he was "luckier than other victims".

But no job was forthcoming. Finally, despite his family's Tolstoyan principles and his own loathing of war, Rosenberg's ambivalent desire to make himself economically self-sufficient impelled him, "with no more free will than a tree", to join up. He would receive a shilling a day and in addition he believed his mother would receive a separation allowance from the Government, though he scarcely fulfilled the criterion of having provided regular financial support for a reasonable period of time.

7

Soldier

I wanted to join the RAMC as the idea of killing upsets me a bit, but I was too small.

I.R.

At the end of October, Rosenberg went to Whitehall and enlisted in the army. Although he understood his family would have to know, he withheld the news, fearing the distress it would produce. When he did eventually write, he placated his parents with the white lie that he had signed on for "home service only". The pressing need for infantrymen had driven the government to recruit cannon fodder into 'Bantam Battalions'. Bantams were named after the small, sturdy fighting cock, and initially drawn from men who were short in stature, yet tough and strong. But by the time Rosenberg joined the 12th Battalion of the Suffolk Regiment, part of the newly-created 40th Division, the criteria had been relaxed. Recruits were now taken from those "whose general physique was obviously unequal to the strain of military service". He found himself among a motley crew of inadequates, "a horrible rabble – Falstaff's scarecrows were nothing to these," he wrote to Marsh, "three out of every four have been scavengers, the fourth is a ticket of leave". In fact, over 80% of a thousand new recruits were weeded out before the battalion saw active service. Rosenberg, with his weak chest, tendency to day-dream, unpolished buttons (often done up in the wrong buttonholes) and anti-authoritarian personality, wasn't one of them.

Equipped with the suit on his back, a comb, a handkerchief, a copy of John Donne's poems and Sir Thomas Browne's *Religio Medici*, the spiritual testament of a seventeenth-century doctor, Rosenberg was sent to Bury St Edmunds for training. He wasn't the ideal recruit, but then nor were any of the others. He had to wait weeks for his uniform and kit to arrive and to subsist on meagre rations. He had to "eat out of a basin together with some horribly smelling scavenger who spits and sneezes into it", and he was under the immediate command of "a little impudent schoolboy pup" who had taken agin him – possibly for anti-Semitic reasons. Sir Thomas' Christian principles that invoked "the general charity I owe unto humanity, as rather to hate than pity Turkes, Infidels, and (what is worse) Jewes", appeared to be of little comfort.

Rosenberg was issued with boots and either wasn't told or didn't pay attention to advice on how to soften the leather with oil, consequently he was in agony on long route marches. He developed swollen feet and "a hole" about an inch round in his heel that probably caused him to trip over during a running exercise in front of the Colonel. He ended up in hospital with severely cut hands under the care of a Major Devoral – "a ridiculous bullying brute" of a doctor. Schiff sent money that he spent on new boots, "shaves and suppers". He also sent water-colours that Rosenberg used to capture his comrades' likenesses and cigarettes that he shared with them. Marsh sent chocolates and Miss Seaton sent books. Extraordinarily, within a month, he had come to value his military life, writing to Marsh, "I don't object to severe duties or menial and filthy work as it hardens me", and to Schiff, "One might succumb, be destroyed – but one might also (and the chances are even greater for it) be renewed, made larger, healthier". It was as if he felt the need for some searing experience that would catalyse a moral and artistic regeneration. In this elevated mood he composed 'Marching (As Seen From The Left File)', a poem that surely encapsulates both the seductive aesthetic of military power and horrifying violence of mechanised war:

> My eyes catch ruddy necks
> Sturdily pressed back—
> All a red brick moving glint.
> Like flaming pendulums, hands
> Swing across the khaki—
> Mustard-coloured khaki—
> To the automatic feet.
>
> We husband the ancient glory
> In these bared necks and hands.
> Not broke is the forge of Mars;
> But a subtler brain beats iron
> To shoe the hoofs of death,
> (Who paws dynamic air now).
> Blind fingers loose an iron cloud
> To rain immortal darkness
> On strong eyes.

Rosenberg seemed to be a magnet for bureaucratic nightmares. Before enlisting he had submitted three works to The New English Art Club and in the autumn he heard that they had been accepted. The letter was addressed to Isaac Bomberg! At Christmas he returned home on four days leave to discover that not only had his mother never received the separation allowance, but the three shillings and six pence per week deducted from his pay, half the total amount, had not been passed on to her. Marsh helped him sort out the problem. Then in January he lost five shillings in the post. During the course of his training he was transferred through two regiments and received three different army numbers, finally becoming Private 22311 in the Eleventh King's Own Royal Lancasters. Rosenberg's identity as a 'special case' had been constructed from earliest times and was particularly resistant to erosion by military culture. No matter what the external deprivations, he strove to establish this, and once established he always felt better. But he needed to do it without provoking envy from his peers or hostility from those in authority. He had previously written to Schiff, "I shall find out the name of the Colonel before I send this letter. Of course if some kind of sense of difference could be established between myself and the others, not that my sensitiveness should not be played upon but only that unnecessary trouble shouldn't be started".

By early 1916 he had succeeded. Despite having been transferred to the Twelfth South Lancashires based near Aldershot, a regiment deprived of adequate rations and full of "the most unspeakably filthy wretches", he was now "known as a poet and artist", and the second in command was a Jewish officer who "knows of me from his people". He had further reason to be pleased. Rodker had submitted 'Marching' to Harriet Monroe, characterising Rosenberg's poems as "rare and remarkable gems". She agreed to publish it in *Poetry* with minor editorial changes that Rodker effected on his friend's behalf.

However, in a less positive assessment of military life the following March, Rosenberg wrote to Lascelles Abercrombie, "Believe me the army is the most detestable invention on this earth and nobody but a private in the army knows what it is to be a slave". Rosenberg's life as a slave was at least partially self-inflicted, he had been offered promotion and turned it down, preferring to remain a private soldier. If he harboured murderous feelings toward his superiors, "these wishes that hide themselves even from ourselves", they must have been channelled into the writing of 'Moses', a verse drama loosely based on the story recounted at the beginning of Exodus, where Moses kills an Egyptian taskmaster whom he sees beating a Hebrew slave – an event that marks his transformation from Egyptian prince to leader of the Hebrew people. In Rosenberg's version, influenced by a wacky plot line suggested by Cohen, the story is set in a time of famine. The slaves have their molar teeth removed by

Pharaonic edict in order to prevent them from masticating food. In an affront to Abinoah the overseer, Moses first sleeps with his daughter Koelue and subsequently suffocates her father by bending back his neck. Beneath the action of the poem like serious thoughts "buried in light words" runs an examination of racial exploitation, sexual politics, power and the roots of revolution.

Rosenberg devoted every minute of his spare time to 'Moses' and more, for he was caught absent-mindedly failing to carry out orders while composing verse in his head and duly punished. By May, when he had a period of six days leave, the work was finished. He and Cohen prepared it for the press. Cohen covered the cost, ever optimistic that he would recoup the money from sales. He created his own imprint, 'Paragon Printing Works', in order to bring out the book in both hardback and paperback editions. It may have been the only publication that Paragon ever produced. When conscription was introduced, Russian-Jewish refugees of military age had to choose whether to serve with the British Army or return to the Russian one. Cohen chose Russia and is not known to have returned.

Writing in 1968, the critic and poet Philip Hobsbaum considered 'Moses' a masterpiece demonstrating Rosenberg's extraordinary handling of plot, use of association and strikingly original diction. He was an important influence, Hobsbaum wrote, on modern poets such as Ted Hughes, Peter Redgrove and Jon Silkin. But fifty years earlier, Marsh could only see a curate's egg. It was "an outrage on humanity that the man who could write the Koelue speech should imbed it in such a farrago":

> Ah! Koelue!
> Had you embalmed your beauty, so
> It could not backward go,
> Or change in any way,
> What were the use, if on my eyes
> The embalming spices were not laid
> To keep us fixed,
> Two amorous sculptures passioned endlessly?
> What were the use, if my sight grew,
> And its far branches were cloud-hung,
> You, small at the roots, like grass.
> While the new lips my spirit would kiss
> Were not red lips of flesh,
> But the huge kiss of power.
> Where yesterday soft hair through my fingers fell
> A shaggy mane would entwine,

> And no slim form work fire to my thighs.
> But human Life's inarticulate mass
> Throb the pulse of a thing
> Whose mountain flanks awry
> Beg my mastery—mine!
> Ah! I will ride the dizzy beast of the world
> My road—my way.

As for the rest, he wished that Rosenberg would pay a little attention to form and tradition. "He seems to me entirely without architectonics," he wrote to Bottomley, "both the shaping instinct and the reserve of power that carries a thing through. It's the same in his painting, he does a good sketch of a design and leaves it there". Bottomley had told Rosenberg that 'Moses' was a prodigious advance saying:

> It is not only that it has so much the sureness of direction of which I have just been speaking, but it has the large fine movement, the ample sweep which is the first requisite of great poetry ... Such speeches as 'Ah Koelue! / Had you embalmed your beauty' and 'I am sick of priests and forms' ... are the very top of poetry, and no one ever did better ...

However in response to Marsh he wrote, "I told him I thought it was worth his while to be intelligible and that an especial obligation is on a dramatic poet to meet his audience at least half-way". He added "In *Moses* I felt some assurance that in him, at last, has turned up a poet *de longue haleine* [of long breath] among the youngsters". Rosenberg couldn't have been more right when he commented to Schiff, "I am afraid my public is still in the womb".

Like many if not all poets, Rosenberg recycled images and selected words from his own peculiar hoard, that would appear over and again in different poems. 'Moses' contains some of his favourites – "roots", "rats", "queer", "droll", "veins", "ghastly" or "aghast", "whim", "bowels", the colour "white", "dust", would all reconverge in his later and most anthologised poem, 'Break Of Day In The Trenches'. The jumble of images in 'Moses' and abrupt changes in register and form that so offended Marsh, are not hurtful to the modern ear. Indeed "Three sheep, your breasts, / And my head between, / Grazing together / On a smooth slope", with its echo from the 'Song of Songs', is a welcome balm to the tirade that precedes it in Moses' early speech:

I am sick of priests and forms,
This rigid dry-boned refinement.
As ladies' perfumes are
Obnoxious to stern natures,
This miasma of a rotting god
Is to me.
Who has made of the forest a park?
Who has changed the wolf to a dog?
And put the horse in harness?
And man's mind in a groove?

Of course one cannot derive a logical narrative from Rosenberg's verse, one cannot reorganise the words to remove contradictions without destroying its poetic power. If the voice in the poem is "sick of priests and forms" that are stiff, dead and dried up like a skeleton, one might ask why the same voice (if it is the same voice) objects to the distinctly unstiff, vaporous, "miasma" of a rotting god, and finds this vapour obnoxious, as ladies' perfumes are to stern natures, thus appearing to characterise itself as a "stern nature". And again, it is clear that it can only be man who has manicured parks, domesticated wolves and tamed horses, yet it is the rotting god who seems to be at fault. Is it god or the priests who have put man's mind in a groove? Are the priests Egyptian oppressors of the Israelites or do they represent the forces of conservatism in Jewish tradition? Is it man or God who is responsible for war? One can only experience the complex emotional mix to which this verse play gives expression.

On Thursday 25th May the 40th Division was inspected by King George V before it left for France. He was apparently impressed with the men's performance, informing the Divisional Commander that the Parade was "quite the best witnessed on Laffans Plain since the outbreak of the war". Rosenberg's, perhaps more brutally honest account of the day stated, "The King inspected us Thursday. I believe it's the first Bantam Brigade been inspected. He must have waited for us to stand up a good while. At a distance we look like soldiers sitting down, you know, legs so short".

A few days later the Division began its embarkation and at the last opportunity, Rosenberg informed his sister, Annie, that he was going. She rushed to the camp where they were able to speak through the perimeter wire. She remonstrated hopelessly with him for some time, begging for a chance to plead his case with the medical officer. She asked him how much money he had and he replied "One Shilling". She had no idea what use he might put it to, but she gave him a further ten shillings. His battalion was scheduled to leave the following day. After an eight-hour crossing it arrived at Le Havre in the early morning of 3rd June 1916. Rosenberg rendered the experience into poetry:

The Troop Ship

Grotesque and queerly huddled
Contortionists to twist
The sleepy soul to a sleep,
We lie all sorts of ways
But cannot sleep.
The wet wind is so cold,
And the lurching men so careless,
That, should you drop to a doze,
Wind's fumble or men's feet
Are on your face.

8

Western Front

We spend most of our time pulling each other out of the mud.

I.R.

The Western Front stretched nearly 500 miles from Switzerland to the Channel coast of Belgium. Millions of soldiers were entrenched along both sides with an area of 'No Man's Land', sometimes as narrow as thirty yards, separating the armies. Behind the front line that was protected with the newly-employed military technology of 'barbed wire', were backup trenches where reserve forces could be held in readiness for combat; dugouts were excavated in the trench walls that provided cramped space for shelter and sleep. And behind the trenches were supply depots, field hospitals and military headquarters. Intensive fighting did not occur everywhere at the same time, but the threat of death from poison gas, sniper fire, heavy artillery or unexpected raiding parties, was ever present. Small stretches of ground were lost and retaken repeatedly at terrible cost, while the remaining soldiers continued their daily life against the bizarre 'normality' of dead bodies, mud, rats, lice and boredom. Into this Dantean landscape was projected Private Isaac Rosenberg, A. Coy 11th(S) Batt. K.O.R.L, British Expeditionary Force, who, not surprisingly, had lost all his socks before leaving England.

One thing that enabled soldiers to preserve a sense of connection with the world they had left behind was an efficient postal service. On average letters took no more than two days to get between the 'Home Front' and the Western Front. Rosenberg was able to communicate with family, friends and patrons. He was able to receive parcels and to submit work to Harriet Monroe in Chicago. Albeit the censor forbade him to send poems home because he couldn't "be bothered with going through such rubbish", Rosenberg took no notice. There are eighty published letters that date from the twenty-two months he spent in the trenches, and there were certainly others no longer extant. His holographs written on scraps of muddied paper arrived home regularly where his sister Annie lovingly typed them out and returned them for further editing. Shortly after arriving in France he wrote Miss Seaton, "I've been in trouble with bad heels; you can't have the slightest conception of what such an apparently trivial thing means. We've had shells bursting two yards off, bullets whizzing all over the show, but all you are aware of is the agony of your heels ... "

Rosenberg's mother sent socks and underwear, Miss Seaton sent novels, Schiff sent newspapers and books, even Mrs Cohen unexpectedly sent him a volume of poems she had herself published. In a physical environment fraught with danger, it is no exaggeration to suggest that Rosenberg owed his psychological survival to the power of poetry. But he paid for his dreamy preoccupation, being frequently punished for unsoldierly conduct, on one occasion for forgetting to put on his gas mask. His chances of living nearly two years would have been severely diminished, were it not for the intervention of his family, who asked Marsh to use his influence in order to get Isaac posted away from the front line.

Plato objected to poetry on the grounds that it undermined young men's courage by giving expression to emotions, to "weakness". Percy Bysshe Shelley, however, believed that poetry had a transformative effect, an enabling function that in a secret alchemy allowed "the poisonous waters that flow from death through life" to be converted into "potable gold". Rosenberg's attitude was nearer to Shelley's. He saw poems as vehicles for the modulation and expression of everyday experience. Poetry was a metamorphic process that forged new forms from the nexus of inner and outer worlds. His commitment to his art surmounted all other concerns. "I will not leave a corner of my consciousness covered up," he wrote to Laurence Binyon, "but saturate myself with the strange and extraordinary new conditions of this life, and it will all refine itself into poetry later on". Painful experience could be tolerated, even valued, as the material out of which poems were made. 'Break of Day in the Trenches', was written soon after he arrived in France and 'Dead Man's Dump', perhaps the most harrowing poem to emerge from the war, derived from his duties as a Royal Engineer almost a year later.

Repair of barbed wire defences was carried out under cover of night. It involved moving mule-carts packed with wire coils and metal stakes up to the front line, and on into no-man's-land. One macabre consequence was the likelihood of running over dead bodies. "I wrote a poem about some dead Germans lying in a sunken road where we dumped our wire," he told Bottomley, "I have asked my sister to send it on to you, though I think it commonplace". In fact Rosenberg had made a truly awesome poem. Although there are nods to Keats and recurrences of his favourite words – "sceptres", "veins", etc. – his distinctive language transcends them. Laden with poetic tropes in a chaos of arresting images, crucifixion allusions, empathy with the enemy, end-rhyme, internal rhyme, visual rhyme, anaphoric repetitions and broken rhythms, the poem graphically conveys the human devastation in which he was mired. The first two stanzas lead us into a work of unprecedented candour – no other poet had given such an arresting close-up before:

> The plunging limbers over the shattered track
> Racketed with their rusty freight,
> Stuck out like many crowns of thorns,
> And the rusty stakes like sceptres old
> To stay the flood of brutish men
> Upon our brothers dear.
>
> The wheels lurched over sprawled dead
> But pained them not, though their bones crunched,
> Their shut mouths made no moan,
> They lie there huddled, friend and foeman,
> Man born of man, and born of woman,
> And shells go crying over them
> From night till night and now.

Rosenberg portrays the earth as waiting impatiently to receive dead souls, their containing bodies – strewn on the ground like empty sacks. Lines like:

> Somewhere they must have gone,
> And flung on your hard back
> Is their souls' sack,
> Emptied of God-ancestralled essences.
> Who hurled them out? Who hurled?'

(stanza 4)

and:

> His shook shoulders slipped their load,
> But when they bent to look again
> The drowning soul was sunk too deep
> For human tenderness

(stanza 8)

compare with the best of Gerard Manley Hopkins, although it is unlikely that Rosenberg had seen his work.

In Rosenberg's finely crafted poem 'Returning, We Hear The Larks', the relief at being still alive at the end of a night's work in no-man's land is tempered by the knowledge that arriving back at the trenches offers only relative safety. But it is not as the title might suggest, a romantic celebration of lark song. Unlike Shelley's skylark whose voice is:

> Like a high-born maiden
> In a palace-tower,
> Soothing her love-laden
> Soul in secret hour
> With music sweet as love, which over-
> flows her bower

Rosenberg's bird 'drops' its song:

> Like a blind man's dreams on the sand
> By dangerous tides,
> Like a girl's dark hair for she dreams no ruin lies there,
> Or her kisses where a serpent hides.

In a thoroughly modernist and strikingly original treatment of the subject, he has taken the objective danger in his environment and fused it with the deeply-felt internal danger that derives from his dread of woman. But there is an ambiguity, the girl herself may be equally at risk, or at least is exonerated from blame, for she is unaware of what her dark hair conceals, "dreams no ruin lies there".

The theme is also elaborated in 'Daughters of War' of which there are seven different versions. Rosenberg considered it his best poem. He worked on it from autumn 1916 and completed the final draft the following year. It deals with the two principle preoccupations of most writers and probably all soldiers – sex and death. Once again, in line with his ambivalent bonding to women, he constructs a mythical scenario in which immortal Amazonian maidens force the souls out of dead male bodies in order to take them for lovers:

> Even these must leap to the love heat of these maidens
> From the flame of terrene days
> Leaving grey ashes to the wind—to the wind.

"The end," he wrote Marsh in June 1917, "is an attempt to imagine the severance of all human relationship and the fading away of human love". No doubt it was a way of using art to come to terms with his situation. Personifying a sexualised soul engaged with an Amazon in some kind of sensual afterlife, "both spiritual and voluptuous at the same time", was a strange yet comforting phantasy. But Rosenberg certainly didn't believe in it. In reality he was more inclined to Lucretius' views, written around 50BC, "That in true death there is no second self / Alive and able to sorrow for self destroyed". R.C. Trevelyan had sent him a copy of his translation of the Roman poet, to which Rosenberg responded, "Hamlet's enquiring nature so mixed with theology, superstition, penetration, may be more human and general – But Lucretius as a mood, definite, is fine, proud philosophy. I can say no more than that I got deep pleasure from it".

On 14th September 1917, having had a bath behind the lines and been issued with a clean uniform, Rosenberg set off for a period of ten days leave in London. He was keen to be reunited with family and friends, hoped to meet Bottomley and Trevelyan, with whom he had only ever corresponded, and wanted to complete 'The Unicorn', an extraordinary verse play about a decaying race who had never seen women. Animals take the place of women, he explained to Bottomley, but the race yearns for continuity. The plot that could only have been devised by a sex-starved soldier would end with "a host of blacks on horses, like centaurs and buffaloes", each one clasping a woman, rushing up and sweeping Lilith on to the Chief's Unicorn; after which they would all ride away into the distance. The fantastical storyline, however, conceals a profound struggle on Rosenberg's part to reconcile war experience with belief in the redemptive nature of beauty, sexual violence with sexual love:

LILITH
I think there is more sorrow in the world
Than man can bear.

NUBIAN
None can exceed their limit, lady.
You either bear or break.

LILITH
Can one choose to break? To bear,
To wearily bear in misery.
Beauty is this corroding malady.

NUBIAN
Beauty is a great paradox—
Music's secret soul creeping about the senses
To wrestle with man's coarser nature.
It is hard when beauty loses.

But the abrupt change of environment was disorientating. Rosenberg found himself restless, unable to read or write and bewildered by the prospect of fitting so many things into such a brief respite. He had his photograph taken in a studio together with his brother Elkon who was also on leave from the army. Bottomley and Trevelyan were away and Schiff was out when he called. Nonetheless he continued to make a round of his old haunts, the Slade, the Café Royal, and managed to meet up with Marsh. He went to the theatre and may have seen Annetta and Sonia. He was on a high, so much so that his withdrawn character appeared radically changed. Leftwich who was hailed by him in the street later recalled:

> I was walking along the road when I heard someone running behind me [...] it was Rosenberg in uniform. He had been on a bus going home from the station to see his mother and he had caught sight of me and had jumped off [...] He was more boisterously happy than I had ever known him before, and he was noisily indignant because he had heard that some people had been saying that he hated the army and wanted to wangle his way out. It was not true, he clamoured. He liked the life and the boys, and he had to fight.

Soon after returning to the front, however, Rosenberg caught the flu. His condition was severe enough to warrant hospitalisation for a period of two months, during which time his regiment was engaged in attacking German defences in the battle of Cambrai, with heavy losses. Any luck he felt at having "got out of this late stunt", was to be short lived. By January 1918 he was back in the wintry trenches with a broken spirit. "I seem powerless to compel my will to any direction," he wrote Miss Seaton, "all I do is without energy and interest". Three weeks later he continued, "I do not feel that I have much to say, but I know that unless I write now it will be a long time before you hear from me again".

In the early hours of 1st April after a period of heavy fighting, he was on his way back to the reserve trenches when he answered a call for volunteers to return to the front line, and was killed in close combat. Ten years later, the Imperial War Graves Commission located an unmarked grave near Fampoux, in which the remains of several soldiers on the same burial list as Rosenberg were identified. In October 1928 they were reinterred in the Bailleul Road East Cemetery, St. Laurent-Blangy, near Arras. A stone bearing Rosenberg's name underneath a Star of David was erected. The words 'Artist and Poet' also appear, for which extra engraving the Commission charged his family three shillings and threepence.

Conclusion

Simple ***poetry****—that is where an interesting complexity of thought is kept in tone and right value to the dominating idea so that it is understandable and still ungraspable.*

I.R.

Rosenberg received scant recognition while he was alive. Even his principal patron, Marsh, only included one example of his work in five volumes of Georgian poetry. He thought of him more as a painter than a poet. The charges against him were "obscurity" and "bad taste", (as well as the more minor infringements of grammar, punctuation and spelling). In his introductory memoir to the 1922 edition of *Poems by Isaac Rosenberg*, Binyon talked of "The obscurities, the straining and tormenting of language in the effort to find right expression, the immaturities of style and taste". Yeats declined to write a foreword to the *Complete Works* published fifteen years later, because he found Rosenberg's verse "all windy rhetoric". Yet the distinguished Cambridge critic F.R. Leavis reviewing the same edition, hailed Rosenberg as a genius whose astonishing spiritual strength, force of originality, and technical skill deserved credit for maintaining the life of the English language. T.S. Eliot admired his work and Keith Douglas' Second World War poem 'Desert Flowers' famously reads: "Rosenberg I only repeat what you were saying".

Clarity of expression is not of itself a virtue. As Veronica Forrest-Thompson indicated in her brilliant 1978 study, *Poetic Artifice*, we might expect a poem to do something more than a piece of prose. Discourse that is immediately accessible or even capable of being made so by a process of critical "naturalisation", may leave poetry "stranded on the beach of the already-known world". In order to go further, and Rosenberg constantly strove to do so, the non-semantic levels of pattern, metre, rhythm, sound and syntax must be brought into play. The complex 'meaning' or 'experience' that the poem then generates remains incapable of reduction. It cannot be easily explained or translated.

Rosenberg's was a unique voice and he worked hard at training it. One can see the process of development in the sequence of his drafts. He wanted to penetrate beneath the surface of things. He was as much a love poet as a war poet, a "real" poet as the Whitechapel Boys had recognised, not a lightweight versifier. To point to his internal conflict is not to lessen the social, political and theological commentary found in his work, or its artistic value. But one cannot help thinking that his struggles on paper, at first with an untrustworthy God and later a positively malign and female one, are linked with his vulnerability to melancholy. Rosenberg's God is also his own bullying superego or persecuting "bad internal object". Reflecting on his life, Joseph Cohen remarks that he was someone who relished the role of the fool but was, in fact, not one. If, as Cohen suggests, he presents the image of a "gifted clown" for whom everything could have gone right but inevitably went wrong, he must also represent the existential plight of all men.

Selected Additional Poems

Zion

She stood—a hill-ensceptred Queen,
  The glory streaming from her;
While Heaven flashed her rays between,
  And shed eternal summer.

The gates of morning opened wide
  On sunny dome and steeple.
Noon gleamed upon the mountain-side
  Thronged with happy people.

And twilight's drowsy, half closed eyes
  Beheld that virgin splendour
Whose orbs were as her darkening skies
  And as her spirit, tender.

Girt with that strength, first born of right,
  Held fast by deeds of honour,
Her robe she wove with rays more bright
  Than heaven could rain upon her.

Where is that light—that citadel?
  That robe with woof of glory?
She lost her virtue and she fell,
  And only left her story.

1906

A Ballad Of Whitechapel

God's mercy shines,
And our full hearts must make record of this,
For grief that burst from out its dark confines
Into strange sunlit bliss.

I stood where glowed
The merry glare of golden whirring lights
Above the monstrous mass that seethed and flowed
Through one of London's nights.

I watched the gleams
Of jagged warm lights on shrunk faces pale.
I heard mad laughter as one hears in dreams,
Or Hell's harsh lurid tale.

The traffic rolled,
A gliding chaos populous of din.
A steaming wail at doom the Lord had scrawled
For perilous loads of sin.

And my soul thought,
'What fearful land have my steps wandered to?
God's love is everywhere, but here is naught
Save love His anger slew.'

And as I stood
Lost in promiscuous bewilderment,
Which to my mazèd soul was wonder-food,
A girl in garments rent

Peered 'neath lids shamed,
And spoke to me and murmured to my blood.
My soul stopped dead, and all my horror flamed
At her forgot of God.

Her hungered eyes,
Craving and yet so sadly spiritual,
Shone like the unsmirched corner of a jewel
Where else foul blemish lies.

I walked with her
Because my heart thought, 'Here the soul is clean,
The fragrance of the frankincense and myrrh
Is lost in odours mean.'

She told me how
The shadow of black death had newly come
And touched her father, mother, even now
Grim-hovering in her home,

Where fevered lay
Her wasting brother in a cold bleak room,
Which theirs would be no longer than a day,
And then—the streets and doom.

Lord! Lord! dear Lord!
I knew that life was bitter, but my soul
Recoiled, as anguish-smitten by sharp sword,
Grieving such body's dole.

Then grief gave place
To a strange pulsing rapture as she spoke,
For I could catch the glimpses of God's grace,
And desire awoke.

To take this trust,
And warm and gladden it with love's new fires,
Burning the past to ashes and to dust
Through purified desires.

We walked our way.
One way hewn for us from birth of Time.
For we had wandered into Love's strange clime
Through ways sin waits to slay.

Love's euphony,
In Love's own temple that is our glad hearts,
Makes now long music wild deliciously,
Now Grief hath used his darts.

Love infinite,
Chastened by sorrow, hallowed by pure flame—
Not all the surging world can compass it,
Love—love—O! tremulous name.

God's mercy shines.
And my full heart hath made record of this.
Of grief that burst from out its dark confines
Into strange sunlit bliss.

1910

Midsummer Frost

A July ghost, aghast at the strange winter,
Wonders, at burning noon, (all summer seeming),
How, like a sad thought buried in light words,
Winter, an alien presence, is ambushed here.

See, from the fire-fountained noon there creep
Lazy yellow ardours towards pale evening,
To thread dark and vain fire
Over my unsens'd heart,
Dead heart, no urgent summer can reach.
Hidden as a root from air or a star from day;
A frozen pool whereon mirth dances;
Where the shining boys would fish.

My blinded brain pierced is,
And searched by a thought, and pangful
With bitter ooze of a joyous knowledge
Of some starred time outworn.
Like blind eyes that have slinked past God,
And light, their untasked inheritance,
(Sealed eyes that trouble never the Sun)
Yet has feel of a Maytime pierced.
He heareth the Maytime dances;
Frees from their airy prison, bright voices,
To loosen them in his dark imagination,
Powered with girl revels rare
And silks and merry colours,
And all the unpeopled ghosts that walk in words.
Till wave white hands that ripple lakes of sadness,
Until the sadness vanishes and the stagnant pool remains.

Underneath this summer air can July dream
How, in night-hanging forest of eating maladies,
A frozen forest of moon unquiet madness,
The moon-drunk haunted pierced soul dies;
Starved by its Babel folly, lying stark,
Unvexed by July's warm eyes.

1914-15

Louse Hunting

Nudes—stark and glistening,
Yelling in lurid glee. Grinning faces
And raging limbs
Whirl over the floor one fire.
For a shirt verminously busy
Yon soldier tore from his throat, with oaths
Godhead might shrink at, but not the lice.
And soon the shirt was aflare
Over the candle he'd lit while we lay.

Then we all sprang up and stript
To hunt the verminous brood.
Soon like a demon's pantomime
The place was raging.
See the silhouettes agape,
See the gibbering shadows
Mixed with the battled arms on the wall.
See gargantuan hooked fingers
Pluck in supreme flesh
To smutch supreme littleness.
See the merry limbs in hot Highland fling
Because some wizard vermin
Charmed from the quiet this revel
When our ears were half lulled
By the dark music
Blown from Sleep's trumpet.

1917

Returning, We Hear The Larks

Sombre the night is.
And though we have our lives, we know
What sinister threat lurks there.

Dragging these anguished limbs, we only know
This poison-blasted track opens on our camp—
On a little safe sleep.

But hark! joy—joy—strange joy.
Lo! heights of night ringing with unseen larks.
Music showering our upturned list'ning faces.

Death could drop from the dark
As easily as song—
But song only dropped,
Like a blind man's dreams on the sand
By dangerous tides,
Like a girl's dark hair for she dreams no ruin lies there,
Or her kisses where a serpent hides.

1917

Dead Man's Dump

The plunging limbers over the shattered track
Racketed with their rusty freight,
Stuck out like many crowns of thorns,
And the rusty stakes like sceptres old
To stay the flood of brutish men
Upon our brothers dear.

The wheels lurched over sprawled dead
But pained them not, though their bones crunched,
Their shut mouths made no moan,
They lie there huddled, friend and foeman,
Man born of man, and born of woman,
And shells go crying over them
From night till night and now.

Earth has waited for them
All the time of their growth
Fretting for their decay:
Now she has them at last!
In the strength of their strength
Suspended—stopped and held.

What fierce imaginings their dark souls lit
Earth! have they gone into you?
Somewhere they must have gone,
And flung on your hard back
Is their souls' sack,
Emptied of God-ancestralled essences.
Who hurled them out? Who hurled?

None saw their spirits' shadow shake the grass,
Or stood aside for the half used life to pass
Out of those doomed nostrils and the doomed mouth,
When the swift iron burning bee
Drained the wild honey of their youth.

What of us, who flung on the shrieking pyre,
Walk, our usual thoughts untouched,
Our lucky limbs as on ichor fed,
Immortal seeming ever?
Perhaps when the flames beat loud on us,
A fear may choke in our veins
And the startled blood may stop.

The air is loud with death,
The dark air spurts with fire
The explosions ceaseless are.
Timelessly now, some minutes past,
These dead strode time with vigorous life,
Till the shrapnel called 'an end!'
But not to all. In bleeding pangs
Some borne on stretchers dreamed of home,
Dear things, war-blotted from their hearts.

A man's brains splattered on
A stretcher-bearer's face;
His shook shoulders slipped their load,
But when they bent to look again
The drowning soul was sunk too deep
For human tenderness.

They left this dead with the older dead,
Stretched at the cross roads.
Burnt black by strange decay,
Their sinister faces lie
The lid over each eye,
The grass and coloured clay
More motion have than they,
Joined to the great sunk silences.

Here is one not long dead;
His dark hearing caught our far wheels,
And the choked soul stretched weak hands
To reach the living word the far wheels said,
The blood-dazed intelligence beating for light,
Crying through the suspense of the far torturing wheels
Swift for the end to break,
Or the wheels to break,
Cried as the tide of the world broke over his sight.

Will they come? Will they ever come?
Even as the mixed hoofs of the mules,
The quivering-bellied mules,
And the rushing wheels all mixed
With his tortured upturned sight,
So we crashed round the bend,
We heard his weak scream,
We heard his very last sound,
And our wheels grazed his dead face.

1917

Daughters Of War

Space beats the ruddy freedom of their limbs—
Their naked dances with man's spirit naked
By the root side of the tree of life,
(The underside of things
And shut from the earth's profoundest eyes).

I saw in prophetic gleams
These mighty daughters in their dances
Beckon each soul aghast from its crimson corpse
To mix in their glittering dances.
I heard the mighty daughters' giant sighs
In sleepless passion for the sons of valour,
And envy of the days of flesh
Barring their love with mortal boughs across—
The mortal boughs—the mortal tree of life.
The old bark burnt with iron wars
They blow to a live flame
To char the young green days
And reach the occult soul; they have no softer lure
No softer lure than the savage ways of death.

We were satisfied of our lords the moon and the sun
To take our wage of sleep and bread and warmth—
These maidens came—these strong ever-living Amazons,
And in an easy might their wrists
Of night's sway and noon's sway the sceptres brake,
Clouding the wild—the soft lustres of our eyes.
Clouding the wild lustres, the clinging tender lights;
Driving the darkness into the flame of day,
With the Amazonian wind of them
Over our corroding faces

That must be broken—broken for evermore
So the soul can leap out
Into their huge embraces.
Though there are human faces
Best sculptures of Deity,
And sinews lusted after
By the Archangels tall,
Even these must leap to the love heat of these maidens
From the flame of terrene days
Leaving grey ashes to the wind—to the wind.

One (whose great lifted face,
Where wisdom's strength and beauty's strength
And the thewed strength of large beasts
Moved and merged, gloomed and lit)
Was speaking, surely, as the earth-men's earth fell away;
Whose new hearing drunk the sound
Where pictures, lutes, and mountains mixed
With the loosed spirit of a thought.
Essenced to language, thus—

'My sisters force their males
From the doomed earth, from the doomed glee
And hankering of hearts.
Frail hands gleam up through the human quagmire,
and lips of ash
Seem to wail, as in sad faded paintings
Far sunken and strange.
My sisters have their males
Clean of the dust of old days
That clings about those white hands
And yearns in those voices sad.
But these shall not see them,
Or think of them in any days or years,
They are my sisters' lovers in other days and years.'

1917

Soldier: Twentieth Century

I love you, great new Titan!
Am I not you?
Napoleon and Caesar
Out of you grew.

Out of unthinkable torture,
Eyes kissed by death,
Won back to the world again,
Lost and won in a breath,

Cruel men are made immortal.
Out of your pain born.
They have stolen the sun's power
With their feet on your shoulders worn.

Let them shrink from your girth,
That has outgrown the pallid days,
When you slept like Circe's swine,
Or a word in the brain's ways.

1917

Girl To Soldier On Leave

I love you—Titan lover,
My own storm-days' Titan.
Greater than the son of Zeus,
I know who I would choose.

Titan—my splendid rebel—
The old Prometheus
Wanes like a ghost before your power—
His pangs were joys to yours.

Pallid days arid and wan
Tied your soul fast.
Babel cities' smoky tops
Pressed upon your growth

Weary gyves. What were you,
But a word in the brain's ways,
Or the sleep of Circe's swine?
One gyve holds you yet.

It held you hiddenly on the Somme
Tied from my heart at home.
O must it loosen now? I wish
You were bound with the old gyves.

Love! you love me—your eyes
Have looked through death at mine.
You have tempted a grave too much.
I let you—I repine.

1917

Further Reading

Poetry and Letters

Isaac Rosenberg: 21st-Century Oxford Authors, ed. Vivien Noakes (Oxford University Press, 2008)

Isaac Rosenberg: Poetry Out of my Head and Heart, ed. Jean Liddiard (Enitharmon, 2007)

The Collected Works of Isaac Rosenberg, ed. Ian Parsons (Chatto & Windus, 1979)

Biographies

Isaac Rosenberg: The Making of a Great War Poet, Jean Moorcroft Wilson (Weidenfeld & Nicholson, 2007)

Journey to the Trenches: The Life of Isaac Rosenberg 1890-1918, Joseph Cohen (Basic Books, 1975)

Criticism

'The Female God of Isaac Rosenberg: A Muse for Wartime', Beth Ellen Roberts, *English Literature in Transition*, 1996, 39, 3, 319-332.

Out of Battle: The Poetry of the Great War, Jon Silkin (Oxford University Press, 1978)

'Fate and the Image of Music: An Examination of Rosenberg's Plays', Charles Tomlinson, *Poetry Nation*, 1974, 3, 57-69.

'Two Poems by Isaac Rosenberg', Philip Hobsbaum, *Jewish Quarterly*, 1969, 61,17,1, 25-29.

'Isaac Rosenberg', Dennis Silk, *Judaism*, 1965, XIV, 4, 463-474.

'The Recognition of Isaac Rosenberg', F.R. Leavis, *Scrutiny*, 1937, VI, 229-234.

'Aspects of the Poetry of Isaac Rosenberg', D.W. Harding, *Scrutiny*, 1934-35, 3, 358-367.

'Introductory Memoir', Laurence Binyon, in *Poems by Isaac Rosenberg*, ed. Gordon Bottomley (William Heinemann, 1922)

GREENWICH EXCHANGE BOOKS

STUDENT GUIDE LITERARY SERIES

The Greenwich Exchange Student Guide Literary Series is a collection of essays on major or contemporary serious writers in English and selected European languages. The series is for the student, the teacher and the 'common reader' and is an ideal resource for libraries. The *Times Educational Supplement* praised these books, saying, "The style of [this series] has a pressure of meaning behind it. Readers should learn from that ... If art is about selection, perception and taste, then this is it."

The series includes:
Antonin Artaud by Lee Jamieson (978-1-871551-98-3)
W.H. Auden by Stephen Wade (978-1-871551-36-5)
Jane Austen by Pat Levy (978-1-871551-89-1)
Honoré de Balzac by Wendy Mercer (978-1-871551-48-8)
Louis de Bernières by Rob Spence (978-1-906075-13-2)
William Blake by Peter Davies (978-1-871551-27-3)
The Brontës by Peter Davies (978-1-871551-24-2)
Robert Browning by John Lucas (978-1-871551-59-4)
Lord Byron by Andrew Keanie (978-1-871551-83-9)
Samuel Taylor Coleridge by Andrew Keanie (978-1-871551-64-8)
Joseph Conrad by Martin Seymour-Smith (978-1-871551-18-1)
William Cowper by Michael Thorn (978-1-871551-25-9)
Charles Dickens by Robert Giddings (987-1-871551-26-6)
Emily Dickinson by Marnie Pomeroy (978-1-871551-68-6)
John Donne by Sean Haldane (978-1-871551-23-5)
Elizabethan Love Poets by John Greening (978-1-906075-52-1)
Ford Madox Ford by Anthony Fowles (978-1-871551-63-1)
Sigmund Freud by Stephen Wilson (978-1-906075-30-9)
The Stagecraft of Brian Friel by David Grant (978-1-871551-74-7)
Robert Frost by Warren Hope (978-1-871551-70-9)
Patrick Hamilton by John Harding (978-1-871551-99-0)
Thomas Hardy by Sean Haldane (978-1-871551-33-4)
Seamus Heaney by Warren Hope (978-1-871551-37-2)
Joseph Heller by Anthony Fowles (978-1-871551-84-6)
George Herbert By Neil Curry & Natasha Curry (978-1-906075-40-8)

Gerard Manley Hopkins by Sean Sheehan (978-1-871551-77-8)
James Joyce by Michael Murphy (978-1-871551-73-0)
Philip Larkin by Warren Hope (978-1-871551-35-8)
Laughter in the Dark – The Plays of Joe Orton by Arthur Burke (978-1-871551-56-3)
George Orwell by Warren Hope (978-1-871551-42-6)
Sylvia Plath by Marnie Pomeroy (978-1-871551-88-4)
Poets of the First World War by John Greening (978-1-871551-79-2)
Alexander Pope by Neil Curry (978-1-906075-23-1)
Philip Roth by Paul McDonald (978-1-871551-72-3)
Shakespeare's *A Midsummer Night's Dream* by Matt Simpson (978-1-871551-90-7)
Shakespeare's *As You Like It* by Matt Simpson (978-1-906075-46-0)
Shakespeare's *Hamlet* by Peter Davies (978-1-906075-12-5)
Shakespeare's *Julius Caesar* by Matt Simpson (978-1-906075-37-8)
Shakespeare's *King Lear* by Peter Davies (978-1-871551-95-2)
Shakespeare's *Macbeth* by Matt Simpson (978-1-871551-69-3)
Shakespeare's *The Merchant of Venice* by Alan Ablewhite (978-1-871551-96-9)
Shakespeare's *Much Ado About Nothing* by Matt Simpson (978-1-906075-01-9)
Shakespeare's Non-Dramatic Poetry by Martin Seymour-Smith (978-1-871551-22-8)
Shakespeare's *Othello* by Matt Simpson (978-1-871551-71-6)
Shakespeare's *Romeo and Juliet* by Matt Simpson (978-1-906075-17-0)
Shakespeare's Second Tetralogy: *Richard II–Henry V*
by John Lucas (978-1-871551-97-6)
Shakespeare's Sonnets by Martin Seymour-Smith (978-1-871551-38-9)
Shakespeare's *The Tempest* by Matt Simpson (978-1-871551-75-4)
Shakespeare's *Twelfth Night* by Matt Simpson (978-1-871551-86-0)
Shakespeare's *The Winter's Tale* by John Lucas (978-1-871551-80-8)
Tobias Smollett by Robert Giddings (978-1-871551-21-1)
Alfred, Lord Tennyson by Michael Thorn (978-1-871551-20-4)
Dylan Thomas by Peter Davies (978-1-871551-78-5)
William Wordsworth by Andrew Keanie (978-1-871551-57-0)
W.B. Yeats by John Greening (978-1-871551-34-1)

FOCUS Series (ISBN prefix 978-1-906075 applies to all the following titles)
James Baldwin: *Go Tell It on the Mountain* by Neil Root (44-6)
William Blake: *Songs of Innocence and Experience* by Matt Simpson (26-2)
Emily Brontë: *Wuthering Heights* by Matt Simpson (10-1)
Angela Carter: *The Bloody Chamber and Other Stories* by Angela Topping (25-5)
Truman Capote: *Breakfast at Tiffany's* by Neil Root (53-8)
George Eliot: *Middlemarch* by John Axon (06-4)
T.S. Eliot: *The Waste Land* by Matt Simpson (09-5)
F. Scott Fitzgerald: *The Great Gatsby* by Peter Davies (29-3)
Michael Frayn: *Spies* by Angela Topping (08-8)

Thomas Hardy: ***Poems of 1912–13*** by John Greening (04-0)
Thomas Hardy: ***Tess of the D'Urbervilles*** by Philip McCarthy (45-3)
The Poetry of Tony Harrison by Sean Sheehan (15-6)
The Poetry of Ted Hughes by John Greening (05-7)
Aldous Huxley: ***Brave New World*** by Neil Root (41-5)
James Joyce: ***A Portrait of the Artist as a Young Man*** by Matt Simpson (07-1)
John Keats: ***Isabella; or, the Pot of Basil, The Eve of St Agnes, Lamia*** **and** ***La Belle Dame sans Merci*** by Andrew Keanie (27-9)
Harold Pinter by Lee Jamieson (16-3)
Jean Rhys: ***Wide Sargasso Sea*** by Anthony Fowles (34-7)
Edward Thomas by John Greening (28-6)
Wordsworth and Coleridge: ***Lyrical Ballads*** **(1798)** by Andrew Keanie (20-0)

Other subjects covered by Greenwich Exchange books
Biography
Education
Philosophy